BEHIND THE
BARBED WIRE

Gwendolyn Chabrier

Orchid Press

Gwendolyn Chabrier
BEHIND THE BARBED WIRE

ORCHID PRESS
G.P.O. Box 13447,
General PO,
Hong Kong
www.orchidbooks.com

Copyright © Orchid Press 2011

Protected by copyright under the terms of the International Copyright Union: all rights reserved. No part of this publication may be reproduced in any form or by any means, electronic or mechanical, including photocopying, recording, or by any information storage or retrieval system without prior permission in writing from the publisher.

ISBN 978-988-18498-1-6

Contents

New York City	1
Pre-War Latvia	3
Germany	15
The Departure of the Volksdeutsche	61
The Russian Occupation	67
The Second World War	75
The Riga Ghetto	89
The Concentration Camps and the Euthanasia Centers	125
Kaiserwald	131
Stutthof	155
Düsseldorf	195
Bibliography	197
About the Author	203

FOREWORD

By Dr Gertrude Schneider

Gwendolyn Chabrier's new book with its focus on World War II in general and the Holocaust in particular, contains an amalgam of luxury and poverty, of old people who were doomed and young people whose zest for living was stronger than their heartache, of utter hopelessness and despair with a childish certainty of survival and of taking vengeance, and above all, of the evil that man can do to those who are defenceless and powerless.

Her skill in describing conditions in Germany and Latvia before and during the war, are sometimes spellbinding. It is hard to put the book down... one wants to know what comes next.

The stories of Hitler and his cohorts and their excesses, whenever she mentions their lifestyle, shows them as degenerates with a lust for blood, mainly Jewish blood, and are extremely well presented; they serve as an eye-opener, even for people who are familiar with the subject.

Chabrier quotes bona fide history from many sources and it is clear that she studied most of what is available, which included visiting the actual killing fields, to enhance her poetic license. At times she even manages to bring a little sunshine to the macabre circumstances, by adding a well-integrated love story. Although the reader knows that there can be no happy ending, the mixture of fact and fiction leaves her audience with a ray of hope. We suffer with the victims, yet we rejoice with the few survivors, who, despite their misfortune, created a new life and are, in the end, victorious.

PREFACE

*B*ehind the Barbed Wire was inspired by a Latvian Jewish friend of mine, George Schwab, the current president of the National Committee on American Foreign Policy in New York City. George, himself, originally from Liepaja was sent to the Liepaja ghetto with his mother and brother in the summer of 1942, after his father was murdered by the Nazis. He was later imprisoned at Kaiserwald Concentration Camp where his brother was killed in a selection under the auspices of the SS Heinz Wisner. Afterwards, George was incarcerated in Stutthof Concentration Camp on the German-Polish border from where he was evacuated with the other inmates a few weeks before the war ended. Immediately following liberation, he was then sent to the Warburg Estate for distressed youth. A year later, George was re-united with his mother and left permanently for the United States where he joined his American relatives. George later married Eleonora Storch, daughter of Hillel Storch, the wartime saviour of thousands of Jewish lives in his capacity as head of the Swedish section of the World Jewish Congress. Thirty-five years ago, I attended in New York City the *bar mitzvah* of George's triplets, which was extremely moving. Storch and many of the most prominent figures of the Holocaust were present and spoke about their experiences during the war. It was then I first wanted to write about George, about his story and the Holocaust.

I have spoken much with him and his friend, Gertrude Schneider, one of the other survivors of the Riga Ghetto, Kaiserwald and Stutthof. Professor Schneider has also written numerous books on the subject. I have furthermore visited Liepaja, Riga,

Kaiserwald and Stutthof in order to acquire a greater understanding of the Holocaust in those areas of Eastern Europe. I have also studied the documentation available on the Liepaja and Riga ghettos, Camp Kaiserwald and Stutthof, as well as consulted numerous works about Hitler and the Nazis as well as the life and conditions in the camps in general in order that this historical narrative could be as credible, innovative, lively and engaging as possible.

Paris, 2010

ACKNOWLEDGMENTS

I would like to thank Dr George Schwab, Dr Gertrude Schneider and Chantal Chawaf, Alain Vircondolet and Fernanda Bruno for their generous help and support, without which this book would not have been possible.

NEW YORK CITY

"Now listen, sir, I'm going to hang up now."

"*Herr* Schwabe! *Herr* Schwabe….hold on!"

"No, I swore to myself I would never again set foot in Germany."

"I understand, but we're talking about the trial of Heinz Wisner himself!"

"Who? Wisner? What, has he been caught?"

"Yes he has, and you understand your testimony is vital for us."

"Oh, my God! Wisner! But how on earth …?"

"After he requested an increase in his social security, we tracked him down with his wife, if you can imagine, enjoying a leisurely vacation at a spa."

"Wisner! The Kaiserwald executioner."

"Yes, Herr Schwabe, I know about your brother."

"Yes, my brother, I owe him that, I owe it to his memory. In the name
of my brother, in the name of my people, I shall come."

"Thank you."

PRE-WAR LATVIA

Doctor, I can only hope that our forthcoming sessions will bring some relief to the excruciating...excruciating pain that gnaws me still. Since my youth, specters haunt me relentlessly, night and day. Otherwise, I wouldn't be here.

Before the outbreak of the war, maybe, ironically, my boyhood in Riga could be considered idyllic. Like many Jews, I came from a very close-knit family. Although my father was a Baltic German and a Lutheran, my mother and her family were Jewish. Both authors and journalists, they traveled often and I, along with my brother and sister, were left with our grandparents and our German governess who was affectionately nicknamed Fräulein. As we grew older, we often accompanied them. Initially, I went to the Latvian school where Jewish boys, like myself, were expected to attend religious classes after school hours and later the Ezra *Schule*, a private Jewish high school. The school was located in a five-story apartment building where the principal also lived. However, its physical facilities were insufficient, the classrooms being so undersized that there was barely space for our wooden desks. At this time, my older brother, Abrasha and younger sister, Svetlana, attended Latvian schools, the girls identifiable through their dark blue skirts and white blouses and the boys recognizable by their military style, black wool tunics and long pants. Both complained constantly that they were ostracized for being Jewish until finally my parents decided that it was necessary to transfer them to a Jewish school. In any case, my family's choices were limited, given that immediately following his coup d'état in 1934, one of President Ulmanis's first decrees specified that minorities were to attend only Latvian schools or one of their own ethnic group.

Otherwise, Ulmanis's fascist government also brought prejudice to the Jews in numerous ways. The Jewish political parties such as the Zionist parties, ZZ-ZS and the *Bund* were liquidated. In the economic arena, the authorities hampered Jewish activities by creating a permit system in all branches of trade and industry. Jewish owners of large factories were also forced to sell them to Latvians, to mention only a few of the reforms which were deleterious to the Jews.

Despite the flagrant anti-Semitism to which we were subjected by everyone, not only the Latvians but also the Russian and the German communities, we still felt honored to be Jewish and forged close ties both in school and in athletics, as well as through the many Jewish or Zionist organizations to which almost all of us belonged. Otherwise, we also had private lessons in English, French, Hebrew, and even in sports.

Following the Soviet annexation, we were taught in Russian; Hebrew was eliminated entirely. Also the Russians forbade any religious observation, including even the morning *Minyan*. Instead, we were indoctrinated in Marxism-Leninism which indisputably became the focal point of our studies. We were taught by a humorless teacher who terrified us as he appeared with a gun bulging from his jacket pocket while he preached to us the works of Marx, Engels, and Lenin.

My mother's family were practicing Jews and we always celebrated the high holidays whether *Rosh Hashanah* or *Yom Kippur*. On *Rosh Hashanah*, we went, for instance, with the other Jewish families down the river for *Tashlik*, the ceremonial dispersal of our sins. For me, this holiday was always upsetting because disputes inevitably broke out with the non-Jews; very often Abrasha and I played with the Gentile boys that timeless game whereby we locked our fingers and tried to bring our opponents to their knees. When we were on the brink of victory, they systematically cried out: "We refuse to kneel before a dirty Jew". We were, once again repulsed and enraged and even fearful of those same cries heard repetitively while attending Latvian school. Apart from the holidays, we furthermore went to *shul*[1] every Friday night and *Shabbat*[2] morning. In fact, my *Bar Mitzvah* was, notwithstanding, the highlight of my boyhood.

It was held at the Gogol *Shul*, the largest and most beautiful synagogue in Riga, known too for its famous singers, cantors, and choir; Rosowsky, Jardlovker, Mandel and Friedland used to sing at the cantor's stand. Even Gentiles came to hear these exceptional cantors.

At thirteen, just before the war, for this long awaited occasion, I was clothed in a dark blue suit and my first pair of long pants. All services were normally conducted by our rabbi, while a cantor was also hired for the holidays and other important services. Often my grandfather expressed his affection for me by covering me lovingly with his prayer shawl. When during my *Bar Mitzvah*, I received my own shawl, he then, with paternal sentiment, pointed to a passage in the *Makzor*[3] in order that I could follow what the cantor was chanting. During these prayers, as during my *Bar Mitzvah*, I would look excitedly through the curtain that divided the women, in their most elegant finery, from the men. During my *Bar Mitzvah*, my grandmother and my mother responded with contentedness and a look of recognition. Svetlana, however, seemed not to have seen me, preoccupied and incommunicative. In any case, all of my family members, including my father, attended. The rabbi called me to the *bima*, the pulpit. I chanted the last part of the weekly *Torah* portion and afterwards the *Haftorah*, the prophetic section that ends the *Torah* reading on the *Shabbat*. Afterwards, the rabbi patted me on the back and congratulated me for my performance. A blushing adolescent, I proudly left the pulpit attended by friends and family.

---

1 Temple
2 Saturday
3 Holiday prayer book

The following day, there was a party at the house, where I again received much praise. The dining room table was covered by a stiff white damask tablecloth and my mother lovingly organized a tea in Russian fashion; that is with slender long spoons. The silver trays were filled with raspberry meringues, apricot turnovers, and glistening red cherries. The tarts were piled with chocolate icing and whipped cream with tiny almond shells and sugar roses in pink and yellow on the mocha glaze. In the background, one could hear the small orchestra consisting of a cellist and a flutist as well as the throbbing sounds of our grand piano. After the congratulatory speeches, we sung many of our favorite Jewish songs. I also received numerous gifts, among them a series of books written by German-Jewish authors, mainly on Jewish and Zionist subjects. Also among my presents, I acquired a radio-receiver, but my favorite was a shiny red bicycle, which I planned to take to the beach for the summer and ride along Jurmala's sand dunes.

How could I even imagine that only a year later, the Gogol *Shul*, the testimonial site of my entry into manhood, would, on 4 July 1941, be burned, along with three hundred refugees from Lithuania who where crowded in the basement. Not to speak of the Jewish families living in the neighborhood, and Jewish passersby, all driven into the synagogue and incinerated alive with the others. After the war, this area became a public garden where a sign, a "Board of Honor", was erected by the Russians, not in commemoration of our tragedy but instead in glorification of the communist "front-rank workers".

Doctor, whenever I remember this I always say kaddish[4] *for the Jews who lost their lives there and especially for those young men who, unlike myself,*

---

4 Prayer for the dead

would never be allowed the same rite of passage into adulthood.

Mr. Schwabe, it is completely normal that you identified with these young boys of your age and that, aware of their tragic destiny, you feel a sense of guilt.

Before the war, however, as I already mentioned, life, at least to me, appeared blissful. In fact, the summers at Jurmala—meaning seaside in Latvian— were particularly memorable. Jurmala, originally a favorite hideaway of Tsarist nobility, is a long ribbon of land between the River Lielupe and the Gulf of Riga. Jurmala consists of a number of villages, among them Majori, Dzintari and Bulduri. We preferred the centrally situated Majori-Dzintari area which had the largest selection of up-market houses, more specifically *dachas,* wooden houses, which always seemed from a distance to resemble gingerbread ones, or at least according to my boyish imagination.

We moved to the beach in the middle of June and back to Riga in mid-August in time for school. The *dachas* were rented furnished, but we brought many of our household supplies, whether cooking utensils or dishes. When I was a young boy in the early 1930's, all of our summer possessions were transported from Riga by horse and cart, later replaced by trucks. Upon arrival at Jurmala, we were required to register with the local police.

In general, whenever Latvian residents moved from one area to another, they were required to report their new abode within a period of two or three days. Mother usually took the summer off and when father occasionally had to leave for an interview or a business trip, she either drove him to the station or accompanied him to Riga in our dilapidated Belgian-made dark green Minerva coupe; the city being less than an hour away. They would usually lunch in Riga in one of the open-air restaurants at the back of the canal. Due to the heat, they ate a light lunch consisting usually of rissoles, with a salad of white cucumbers and tomatoes. Simultaneously, the firemen in their summer leisure hours were spraying the grass in Riga's nearby parks with their hoses.

Before returning to Jurmala, Mother and Father often walked romantically, hand in hand along the canal, which was also the moat initially protecting the original Hanseatic town, whose walls were demolished in the middle of the nineteenth century. Yet, this part of Riga with its cobbled streets nevertheless maintained a timeless charm. It was here that my father's ancestors lived, generations earlier. Like many of the Baltic Germans, his family were merchants and lived in the multi-story houses, whose tiled and garbled roofs also protected the floor below, where the storeroom was located. Our family's homes overlooked the neighboring patrician houses, renowned for their stone portals and chevron built-shutters. Many of them were surrounded by tall trees, whose shade alleviated the summer heat. On the riverfront below, one could see the horse drawn carts, particularly recognizable by their wooden yokes fastened tightly over the horses' heads, transporting various goods for shipment. Their cargo was often added onto small steam ferries and taken to Riga's harbor. Meanwhile, the offices and the shops remained open in summer from eight to three; an exodus of summer commuters left Riga systematically on weekday afternoons and, like my parents, returned to Jurmala.

West of Riga lays the strand, over forty miles of sandy beaches fringed by pine forests and dunes. Excepting the gingerbread pavilion of the old *Kurhaus* at Edinburg and the hydropathical establishment, no building had been allowed to be constructed within close proximity to the sea. Our *dachas*, separated from the sea by a series of imposing dunes, albeit picturesque, were far from functional. Our timber houses had no running water, heat or bathrooms. We were obliged to wash in basins in our bedrooms with cold water carried in large ceramic or enamel ewers from a pump outside the house. When hot water was desired, it was heated on the wood burning range in the kitchen. There were no laundry facilities, thus few clothes were ever washed during summer. We relieved ourselves in the nearby forest where we also picked wild blueberries and mushrooms and brought soap to the beach or the river in order to cleanse ourselves.

Since the Tsarist period, nudism was at a premium. From eight to ten, men could bathe nude before leaving for the city, while from ten to noon the beach was reserved for the women and children under twelve, except for a mixed bathing area existing approximately every five kilometers. However, nude bathing was not permitted during the afternoons or on weekends when the beach was accessible to both sexes. Policemen, known to be chosen for their asexuality, patrolled the beach. Yet, despite that, many men during the women's hours were known to hide excitedly behind the dunes with binoculars. Since sportswear was little known in Latvia at this time, we were often dressed very formally in coats and ties even to go to the beach, always feeling a bit ridiculous. However, in late afternoon, one could see Jurmala's seasonal citizens after returning from work, men promenading nonchalantly down the beach in their sanatorium style pajama suits which resembled fancy sailor suits. While growing up, the beach water and the river had always been crystalline, yet, the many decades of Soviet mismanagement left them polluted, and swimming has thus been discouraged for many years.

In the morning Fräulein often accompanied us to the open-air market, which was not surprisingly smaller than the one in Riga. It consisted of a number of booths and stalls, each of which sold one kind of product, whether meat, fish, dairy, vegetables or fruit. The merchants were born salesmen and loudly and enthusiastically praised their goods. Smoked fish, sardines and small fish were a particular delicacy, and the merchants, like ourselves, bought the fish directly from the fishermen, who smoked their early morning catch in small shacks along the beach not far away from our *dacha*.

Much of our day was also allotted to swimming, diving or tennis. We were taught swimming and diving lessons at the Jewish Yacht Club on the River Lielupe. During our lessons, *Herr* Dubrowsky accompanied us in a dory. He was much more patient with us than our autocratic tennis pro, whom we hated, at *Ritek*, the Jewish Tennis Club. I also have fond memories of the time spent building sand castles or sailing boats at the edge of the sea. Hide and seek was also a favorite activity as was *skach ki*, a game we played in the middle of the street with two sticks, the bigger one usually a broom stick. The rules were numerous and we formed teams and organized competitions against other groups of boys.

The central shopping area was not far from our house and on weekends we jumped on trolley car no. 5 in order to shop; this district being comprised of a candy store, a household goods shop, a bakery, a kosher butcher and a barbershop where we got our hair cut. Bald haircuts were ironically in fashion. The bathhouse was also a few blocks from home. We went there every Friday and the bath was always ritualistically followed by an ice-cream in summer and a *Rubanankus* lemon soda in winter.

Without either telephones or newspapers, we felt as if we were living outside of time. In the Baltic, summer nights are short and the days long, the sun setting after ten. These white nights were mystical as the lofty trees threw a double shadow from the retreating sun and the rising moon. As we sat on the porches of our *dachas*, surrounded by low fences of white pilings and tall, spindly pines, we smelled the lilacs in the evening mist as we heard the sea's rumbling. At that time, I never imagined that war might be approaching and that nearly all of us Latvian Jews were destined for destruction.

In September, we returned to school and to the humdrum of our normal existence. My parents were very active socially and entertained many foreign authors and journalists as well as politicians. Our dining room, as well as the rest of our apartment overlooking Riga's harbor, was decorated with antiques that my parents had bought from the Tsarist palaces when the Russian nobility had placed their furniture and other possessions on sale. This furniture, exclusively in dark wood, seemed unnecessarily massive but the blue and white porcelain baroque chandelier which lit the dining room was not only majestic but filled with whimsy, neither of its branches resembling the other. At one point, when we were very small, my mother and father frequently traveled to Russia in search of these Tsarist treasures, particularly Fabergé eggs, which they collected and shipped back to Riga with their cart loads of furniture.

When we were not submerged by visitors, we resumed our familial intimacy. Our dining room table was often covered by the same white damask tablecloth that Mother had used for my *Bar Mitzvah*, the white and gold china with initials and crests belonging to my great-grandparents, the Russian silver and three cut-glass decanters filled with yellow, gold and pale green liquid. Our meals were also rather formal and dignified events. Father always sat at the head of the table, my mother flanked ceremoniously on his right as she signaled the housekeeper with the crystal buzzer, followed by Abrasha, Svetlana and myself. We each had our own initialed linen napkin in a napkin ring alongside our place setting.

Many of my parents' friends were British and my father was invited frequently to the British Club, known for its refinement. Apparently, the first Thursday of every month the members met for dinner, the club being reputed for its culinary excellence. Additionally, behind each chair stood a waiter—can you imagine—ready to replenish each member's *Kurlände* or king-size vodka glass. Once a year, the wives were also invited to a dinner of hash, known to be rather mediocre, and a pudding, which was clearly inedible. Some thought the club was trying to save money but father was convinced that in keeping with the Anglo-Saxon code, the men desired at all costs to remain among themselves, and this yearly dinner was a means of discouraging their spouses' presence. Latvia might be a long way from

London but Englishmen, like all other nationalities, remain true to themselves.

Otherwise, the social event my parents preferred was the New Year's Ball at the Riga Jewish Club. Father and even Mother were undeniably Aryan in appearance; tall, blond and blue-eyed. For this particular occasion, they always dressed elegantly, Father in a dark tuxedo and black patent leather pumps and Mother always in one of her long gowns, high heels, long gloves, her best jewelry, and a chinchilla stole that my father had given her for their first wedding anniversary. New Year's morning, always a bit tipsy, they returned wearing fancy paper hats and carrying other party favors.

Otherwise, every Sunday, they took us to our favorite restaurant, *Schwarz's Bar* in the basement of the *Hotel de Rome*. The counter was covered with a variety of scrumptious *zakouski* consisting of smoked salmon, red and black caviar, trout, eel, cold meats with mayonnaise and sour cream, hard boiled eggs and ham with dill, salt cucumber and pickled mushrooms, all spread out on small pieces of white, brown or black bread. Vodka was served in glasses of different sizes, each with a specific name. It was furthermore essential to pick the right one, as Latvian etiquette forbade one to sip; all of the glass was expected to be drunk in one gulp, followed immediately by a *zakouski* that awaited us on a fork.

> *Doctor, at times, I may seem completely obsessed by food but never forget that for three, close to four years, four interminable years, I nearly died of starvation, so please bear with me.*
>
> *Your craving for food is a form of compensation.*

Additionally, winter in Latvia, which begins in October and lasts until April, is comprised of very short days and endless nights. It was an enjoyable season for us, because when we were not in school, we were usually sledding or throwing snowballs, often at each other, or if not at passing cars. Many times we also jumped upon the horse drawn sleds to be pulled along the street. Yet, we were most enthused by our day trips to White Lake, a stretch of water lying in the forest beyond the town, where we played hockey or held ice yacht races as soon as the lake would be frozen over. Meanwhile, the Daugava River seemed interminable, starting in Russia and flowing to Latvia, emptying only into the Gulf of Riga and then the Baltic Sea. During the winter season when the river was frozen, ice-cutters cut huge squares of ice to store in warehouses for summer use. At this time of year, farmers would also sled down the river, using it as a road. Nevertheless, it could be quite dangerous, people sometimes falling through the ice. Occasionally, ice floats would also develop and even animals were pathetically stranded on them. In summer, too, there were drownings. More than once, we watched the tugboat fatalistically retrieving the drowned bodies *en route* to the morgue.

Meanwhile, when we were involved in winter sports, Svetlana, who was a very gifted and avid dancer, was spending her free time training for her various performances. Just before the school holidays, we attended with Mother and Father probably the last of her recitals. All the family continued to be mesmerized by her agility and grace. By the time she was nine, she was among the best ballet dancers in Riga.

When the curtain opened that Sunday, in December, we saw on stage the traditional *Chanukah* toy, which, after it was spun, gains or losses of either money, nuts, or raisins, were determined. It consisted of a silver-colored box with a Hebrew letter glued to each of its four sides. As the floodlight passed over the darkened stage, Svetlana's slim body inside, we could only see her head with a matching silver colored hat and on the bottom her silver ballerina shoes. Behind her were four other similar boxes, this time with a gold letter pasted on the side. Visible, too, were only the heads and feet of these younger, smaller girls, now with golden hats and shoes. When the music began, they danced with elegance around the stage in their glittering ballerina costumes, all in unison until the end of the performance, when they toppled to the floor forming a circle around the dancer who stood erect above them. That dancer was none other than Svetlana. The applause echoed throughout the theatre as she bowed and proudly received bouquets of flowers from the spectators in the audience.

Among our privileged moments in wintertime were our visits to our relatives in Liepaja, three or four hours outside of Riga. There, we often attended the tea dances at the Petersburg Hotel with Mother and her sister, Aunt Clara. I must confess that throughout my boyhood, I was a Freudian delight. I was a mother's boy "par excellence", completely infatuated by my cherished mother, thunder struck by her intelligence, gentleness, and beauty. Consequently, at the dances, I tried to monopolize her entirely, and whenever Abrasha, one of my cousins, or worse still, a man of her own age desired to dance with her, I did everything in my power to ward them off, often deliberately tripping my competitors. I recognized that my reactions were absurd, but I could not control them. Like many other boys, I simply wanted my mother all to myself. Equally romantic were our sled rides, snuggling together, as we were driven by horses, their bells jingling in the winter night as they pranced over Liepaja's snow covered cobbled streets. However, we would later learn that these same sleds with bells accompanied by SS and Latvian guards took Aunt Clara and my cousins on their death ride to Skede, the seaside area next to the city, in December 1941. They were told that they were going to be evacuated from Liepaja and to take provisions for three days. At the sea, a half an hour later, they and thousands of other Jews, particularly women and children, after being stripped naked, would be shot in mass killings by the Nazis and their Latvian collaborators, while only the horses attempted to retaliate, bucking and bellowing among the wailing and the gunshots.

GERMANY

Our trips also included fairly frequent voyages to Germany where many of my father's relatives lived. Father also seemed to know Hitler and many of his Nazi entourage. Even Abrasha and I had seen Hitler numerous times. We found him strange, weird, even spooky... He seemed haunted, bewitched... Years later I wondered if he was not possibly the devil incarnate. Meanwhile, many Latvians, also many Jews thought that my father was a Nazi spy. Actually, we, too, thought that he may have been a spy, but we were not sure for whom. We questioned if he may not have pretended to be a Nazi supporter, for his own protection and ours as well. We also surmised that he might even have been clandestinely active in some Nazi resistance movement. Even Mother did not really seem to know. Yet, I will never forget when he learned that Hitler had become chancellor; he went stony faced and did not say a word for the rest of the day.

I had just turned six when I made my first voyage to Germany, to Düsseldorf, in 1932, a few months before Hitler's chancellorship, not knowing that my first and last trip to Germany fifty years later would be to the same city. Albeit I stayed with my German relatives, I had no particular affection for my cousin Joachim. In fact, the more I got to know him, the more I truly detested him. There was also no love lost between myself and my uncle and aunt or my other cousins, Hilda and Günther.

When we arrived in Düsseldorf, Fräulein explained to us that the city was intriguing in the sense that it was a combination of opposites, of a major industrial city on the one hand and a fashion paradise on the other. I remember this also being the case when I returned many years later for the trial. The Königsallee, known as the Kö, one of Germany's most famous streets, was lined on one side with banks and on the other with luxurious boutiques, both shaded by chestnut trees and divided by a many-bridged canal down the center, filled with ducks and swans. Apart from a few stray beggars, the boulevard was peopled with dandified men and elegant but pretentious looking women, haughtily strolling up and down with their poodles, who seemed as well or even better groomed than their mistresses. I wondered as a young boy how many of these cold, stern-looking people were also Nazis like my relatives. I imagined quite a few.

My cousins, however, lived in the *Altstadt*, the older part of town. The baroque-style house was located close to Bolker Street where the poet Heinrich Heine was born and raised. The interior of their home, with its heavy, dark wood was as austere and drab as they themselves. Consequently, we were very pleased when Fräulein would take us to visit the city and we could escape the oppressive atmosphere of their home. In contrast, however, the nearby streets were brimming over with taverns and pubs, many even referring to the *Altstadt* as "the longest bar in the world". Fräulein even took us once to one of the beer taverns where we sipped from her glass Düsseldorf's famous dark colored beer, *altbier*, served to us by a *zappe*, a jolly, blue aproned waiter. Meanwhile, the streets were also booming with the *radschläger*, for which the city was reputed. Apparently, this tradition existed since the eighteenth century. It began at the wedding of Joan Wellen, patron of the arts and the city's elector. During the ceremony, a wheel of his coach became loose and a ten-year-old boy clung to it while cart wheeling until the end of the voyage. We, ourselves, were dying to try out this new sport but Fräulein was afraid we could have an accident and worse still she would be fired.

Actually, Fräulein did almost lose her job on this trip when she took us to mass at *Pfarr-Kirche* St. Andreas, the parish church of St. Andrews, a Baroque post-Jesuit church located also in *Altstadt*. Since historically, abductions of Jewish children by Orthodox clergy and forced baptisms had left a deep imprint on the Jewish psyche, both my mother and my grandparents had always told Fräulein to avoid at all costs taking us to a service in a Christian Church. She took this initiative thinking that one visit would be educational and certainly not deleterious. However, greatly dismayed, the family almost dismissed her.

In any case, Joachim was already, shall we say, a confirmed Nazi and reminded me of all those prejudiced little pricks in our Latvian schools. When one day, I accompanied him to his classes, I found a large swastika flag, a sea of red, dotted with a white circle offsetting the black swastika, projecting from one of the school's turrets at the top of the building. The English teacher, Dr. Bernstein, climbed up the fire escape and removed it with one hand, given that he had lost the other one fighting for Germany during World War I. When we arrived in the classroom, "dirty Jew" was also written on the blackboard. Once again, master of the situation, Dr. Bernstein erased the board and replaced it with "*Maginot* Jew", *maginot* being the slang word for veteran. I later learned that my cousin and his Nazi friends had been entirely responsible for these overt declarations of anti-Semitism. Consequently, I never returned to my relatives' home, but was not surprised to learn that Joachim and Günther had later become active members of the Hitler Youth Movement, as well as almost all their friends.

My brief sojourn of only two weeks in Düsseldorf cured me of Germany for life. Until then having always been protected from anti-Semitism, I returned to Riga completely off balance. Gratuitous hatred was so illogical to me. As a youth, I understood that someone could dislike, even detest somebody or something but there had to be a reason for this. Whenever I had asked Joachim why he hated Dr. Bernstein, why he hated the

Jews, why he even hated me, my cousin could only utter incoherently that 'the Führer said...' that 'the Führer this' or 'the Führer that'.

Years after the war, although I never wanted to return to Germany, no less Latvia, I spoke to many Germans of my generation in New York and read as much as possible about pre-war Germany and its youth in an effort to better understand the incomprehensible. At Harvard in my senior year, I roomed with two other Europeans, one French, the other German. My roommate from Munich, Wolfgang, explained to me how he and his peers had been demonically conditioned by Hitler. He told me that by 1933, Germany's youth were brainwashed into believing that life's sole purpose was to execute the Führer's will, even at the price of their lives. While *Mein Kampf* had replaced the prayer book at school, children systematically and laboriously wrote out the same dictation; one which he still remembered years later:

> *Jesus and Hitler, as Jesus freed me from sin and Hell,*
> *so Hitler freed the German people from destruction.*
> *Jesus and Hitler were persecuted, but while Jesus was*
> *crucified , Hitler was raised to the chancellorship…*
> *Jesus strove for Heaven, Hitler for the German earth.*

In a similar fashion, he also taught me that the League of German Girls[5] developed a new version of the Lord's prayer which was a supplication for Hitler, not only as Germany's leader, but more importantly as its deity:

> *Adolf Hitler, You are our great leader. Thy Third Reich*
> *comes, thy will alone is law upon earth. Let us hear*
> *daily thy voice and order us by thy leadership,*
> *for we will obey to the end even with our lives.*
> *We praise him! Heil Hitler!*

---

5   Or *Jungmädels*; the female Hitler's Youth group

Even very small children, like his younger brother, were not spared and were taught to repeat by rote a prayer adapted to their capacities, which having heard so often, he also had never forgotten:

Führer, my Führer, sent to me from God, protect
and maintain me throughout my life. Thou who hast
saved Germany from deepest need, I thank thee
today for my daily bread. Remain at my side and never
leave me Führer, my Führer, my faith, my light.
Hail, my Führer.

He further showed me that Nazism had also penetrated the essence of family life. His father taught him and the other children to salute him already at the breakfast table with "*Heil Hitler*". Boys of only four, whom they knew, dressed up in SS uniforms and marched around their homes and backyards waving swastika flags. Hitler considered that the masses needed an idol, thus he encouraged that his portrait be placed systematically in nearly every German home. Even children's doll houses like Wolfgang's sister, were adorned with miniature portraits in their living rooms. Postcard pictures of Hitler were also on sale on nearly every street corner; the chancellor's portrait was the centerpiece in the shops' window displays, while the swastika hung over their doors.

Teachers also indoctrinated him and the other German youths in anti-Semitism, proclaiming that we, the Jews, were evil incarnations of the devil, to be spit at and killed. Not surprisingly, in 1938, we were banned entirely from the German schools. Yet, this notwithstanding, we were still expected along with the others to do our "*Heil Hitler*" at least fifty, if not a hundred and fifty times a day. Even their daily prayers ended with "*Heil Hitler*". Wolfgang admitted to me that he never questioned the Nazis; he just obeyed.

I also learned that childhood terminated at ten, when many young Germans entered the *Jungvolk* for boys or the *Jungmädels* for girls, and at fourteen, they continued into the Hitler Youth Movement or the League of German Girls, respectively. Optional initially, by 1936, membership to the National Socialist Youth Movement was mandatory for both sexes over ten.

While sports had previously occupied two hours of a youngster's school week, athletics, being a Nazi obsession, now instead ate up two hours of the children's day. Boxing was encouraged, in particular, since it developed the aggressive spirit and the ability to make quick decisions, both characteristics essential for war. Given Hitler's anti-intellectualism, a result of his own feelings of inadequacy, in his new Reich attention was placed simply on the body, never the mind or the soul. This notwithstanding, he believed, as he earlier expressed in *Mein Kampf*, that the state's primary educational task was to instill in its youth racial consciousness, true to his same obsession. Immediately following his chancellorship, he required that Germany publish a new type of youth book, one glorifying the heroes of the Party and the history of the National Socialist Movement, as well as the life of the martyrs who gave their life for the Nazi cause.

A few of my cousins' friends, however, also like them, stemming from a bourgeois background, resisted Nazi leadership, and were alluded to as the "Swing Youth". These young people, as told by Wolfgang, gathered in pubs and bars as well as private homes where they danced, according to the Nazis, to the "decadent" Jewish and "degenerate" music of Benny Goodman, Tommy Dorsey, Duke Ellington, Louis Armstrong and other stars of the Jazz Age. They were, further, admirers of Anglo-American fashion and culture. In fact, they were in many ways precursors of the hippies, often also long-haired bohemians. Similar to the flower children and unlike Hitler's Youth, they were usually apolitical and ineffectual, so in the final analysis, they created only a limited threat to the National Socialists.

Upon Hitler's appointment, Joachim entered the *Jungvolk* and Günther joined the Hitler Youth Movement.

Joachim as a *Pimpf*[6] was obliged to pass an initiation test, after which he received his first dagger, a highly abridged synthesis of Nazi dogma and the "Horst Wessel Song"[7], and a map-reading exercise for his participation in pseudo war games, much the same ones that occupied Hitler as a young boy at Linz. At age fourteen, Joachim, who was never a brain trust, remained equally illiterate but at least had learned semaphore reading, bicycle repairs, the laying of the telephone wires and small arms drill, and God knows what else; in a word, he and his comrades were already prepared for war. Meanwhile, Günther in April 1933, as was the custom, participated in the ceremony officiating his entry into the *Hitler Jugend*, which was always held on the Fürher's birthday. There, he and thousands of other fourteen-year-old Nazi addicts proudly pledged their undying allegiance to their leader, repeating religiously the following statement:

I consecrate my life to Adolf Hitler;
I am ready to sacrifice my life for Hitler;
I am ready to die for Hitler, my savior, the Führer.

I concluded that Hitler was coming to replace God. I imagined that the German people needed someone to believe in but then so did we, especially now, us, Jews.

Everyone needs to believe in someone or something, Mr. Schwabe, otherwise life would seem, without any purpose.

According to Father, accompanied by their parents and their bovine sister, Gretchen, in May of the same year, both of the boys went to Berlin and participated euphorically in the Nazi's May 10th book burning. In many university towns throughout the country, the

---

[6] A ten to fourteen-year old who was part of the *Jungvolk*
[7] The official anthem of the Nazis, sung after the national anthem "*Deutschland, Deutschland über Alles*"

works of all Jewish writers went up in flames, as well as those condemned by government censure. Bands of Nazi youths broke into the libraries and like bandits stole all the works that Joseph Goebbels, Minister of Propaganda and the Ministry of Propaganda and Public Enlightenment abhorred. In Berlin, dressed in their Hitler Youth uniforms, those suspender-held shorts and dwarf-looking ties, my cousins and their Nazi cronies threw the books into the cars and brought them to Unter den Linden, where the opera house stands impressively, its pedimental portico and winding stairs running on either side as it faces the Humboldt University, the *alma mater* of Heinrich Heine, Karl Marx and Friedrich Engels. Its other side was used for setting the books on fire. Almost twenty thousand authors, including almost every eminent name in modern German letters went up in flames. Numerous foreign authors were also incinerated, among them Upton Sinclair, H.G. Wells, Jack London, André Gide, Emile Zola, and Marcel Proust. The works of scientists such as Albert Einstein and Sigmund Freud were also sacrificed. In the distance, according to my parents who were in Berlin, one could apparently hear my cousins and their Nazi compatriots, like devils, crying out *"Brenne Sigmund Freud"*[8] among other people! However, as they danced around the fire, it was they who were the devils, not us, the Jews.

    Father told us that consequently, thousands of writers, artists, films and theater directors, photographers, stage designers, editors and others who worked for the radio and the press precipitously left Germany. The book burning was justified as self purification. Goebbels who became as of March the new *Gauleiter* of German culture was repaying all the Jews and the "Culture Bolsheviks", who had once rejected his articles and ridiculed his novel. But was not Heine a visionary when he wrote

---

8 Burn Sigmund Freud

"Wherever they burn books, sooner or later they will also burn human beings"?

Later my aunt and uncle, filled with admiration, reported to my parents that when a seven-year-old Jewish boy that my cousins had found outside their school refused to respond to their "*Heil Hitler*" salutes, Joachim and Günther obliged him to take his pants off in the street in order to see whether or not he was circumcised. Later still, in anticipation of *Kristallnacht*, my cousins, along with a group of other boys, all dressed in Hitler Youth uniforms also smashed the windows of a small neighborhood jewelry store and stormed into the shop. While brandishing their butcher knives, screaming at the top of their lungs, "To hell with the Jewish Rabble! Room for the Sudeten-Germans!", they threw everything they could find onto the street, while the others broke glass shelves and anything else they could destroy. After having spit on the owner, my cousins returned with dozens of rings on their fingers and their pockets filled with watches and bracelets, which they lavished on their parents and friends. A few SA men witnessed the scene and with obscene laughter forced the terrified owner to pick up the glass, his hands drenched with blood. The shop owner's passport was also seized, as was often the case, and given over to the president of the police and sold back to its owner for an exorbitant price; Jewish passports could be worth as much as two hundred and fifty thousand marks.

When Father recounted these stories with disgust, Abrasha and I were appalled and only happy to be living in Latvia and not Germany. We never imagined that this could happen in our country.

However, our parents later told us that by the end of 1935, my aunt and uncle, along with many of their contemporaries, became gradually disenchanted with Hitler and specifically with the Hitler Youth. They came to understand that Nazism was simply destroying family life. Baldur von Schirach, whose nobility was as falsified as Ribbentrop's, as Youth leader of the Reich, announced quite simply that "Family life is an old-fashioned concept. We have no need for it, in our new life, which puts the state above all. Don't trust anybody. Watch your wife. Watch your children. Watch everybody. And report their activity to the government."

One day, for example, the boys became incensed because my aunt insisted that they obey her orders, which you would think was only normal. They drew their daggers from their sheaths in an attempt to assault her while chanting methodically "Never forget, we belong to the Führer first! The family comes second. If you want to continue your friendship with our father's family, those Jew devils, we will have to report you." Do you imagine how they came to behave even with their own mother, who before had been raised on a pedestal? Abrasha once asked Father why he told us all these horrible stories about Germany. Was there a reason? Father answered that "knowledge was power." I realized later that he was trying to protect us should we ever be subject to similar prejudice, and God knows we were.

Simultaneously, Father informed us that six-month labor service had become mandatory for girls and many families were trying to avoid it as long as possible, given the risk that their young daughters could return pregnant, birth control being forbidden throughout the Third Reich. My cousin, Gretchen, was not surprisingly a member of the League of German Girls, and like her brothers imbued with Nazidom. Albeit fifty percent of the girls became pregnant during their service, we never expected that Gretchen, obese, gawky and homely would be among those destined for motherhood. She was the epitome of the Valkyrie type, tall and heavy with blond braids and a clean-scrubbed face without ever any make-up. Gretchen was always dressed in matronly fashion in accordance with Nazi dictum; oxfords, a black skirt down to her ankles and a brown jacket with a swastika. Worse yet, my cousin was overjoyed to give birth, telling her parents "I'm proud to be able to give Him (Hitler) a baby. I hope it will be a boy, to die for Him". When my father visited his family in Düsseldorf, she emphatically told him: "under no circumstances call me Gretchen anymore and refrain also from using the familiar "du" when talking to me. I am one of the Führer's brides and do not care to talk to anti-socialists. Worse yet, you're a Jew because you're married to one."

For me, a good Jewish boy from a conservative family, my cousins' rebellion seemed unfathomable. I was also shocked that Gretchen had become pregnant out of wedlock and was only relieved that we were not living in Germany and that Svetlana had not found herself in the same situation.

Furthermore, we understood from Father that Hitler and his Reich were, from its outset, totally misogynous. Not only were there no women in the Nazi government, but the weaker sex was relegated almost inevitably to the home and family; the only allusion to women in the program of the National Socialists was Point 21, pleading protection for mothers. I learned after the war that women were, furthermore, discouraged from working and earned a third less than men. However, before the war, with the increasing need of female labor, the government in 1937 retracted, in spite of themselves, the stipulation stating that marriage loans were only available to non-working women. By 1939, women had even reached thirty-four percent of the German work force.

Father told us, too, that the Führer was otherwise obsessed with procreation, specifically procreation of the Aryan race. Even illegitimate children with the right blood were highly welcomed in the New Reich. Wouldn't Rudolf Hess claim that "Germany needs strong, healthy offspring? A German girl is honored by bearing illegitimate children." Hitler, himself, would further add in an article he wrote for the *Schwarze Korps*: "Try out the future spouse; how else can you tell if the choice is a good one?"

After Father returned from one of his trips to Berlin he discussed with us Germany's social evolution, which seemed completely amazing to all of us. As of then, in 1936, Hitler created *Lebensborn* homes, the first at Steinhöring, outside Munich, where Gretchen and two of her close friends were sent. I could only thank God once again that it was Gretchen and not my sister. The *Lebensborn* homes were maternity homes created by the SS Race and Resettlement Bureau, which were founded mainly for the brides and wives of young SS men and secondly for illegitimate mothers such as Gretchen, considered of very good blood. There, like children, the pregnant women were addressed only by their first names. A sense of Germanic order was maintained and the pregnant mothers were expected to keep their rooms immaculate at all times, despite the few visitors which they were permitted to entertain and their newborn child additionally received its name in a "Germanic cult" ceremony; the Reich's newborn was laid on a pillow before an altar covered with a swastika-emblazoned cloth. A boy was touched on the forehead with an SS "dagger of honor" and inducted into the Black Order. For a girl, one of the SS leaders would make a short speech followed by the ceremonial name giving, which ended with a song, sung by those present.

If a couple could not conceive due to the husband's inability, the wife could report to a specific office alluded to as the *Lebensborn*. This "Fountain of Life" service would put at her disposition a "begetter", also of good Aryan blood. The child born of this extramarital union was considered as legitimate and obliged to be recognized by the mother's husband as his legal child. Every unmarried woman of good breeding who was childless and thirty or over, was also forced to report to the *Lebensborn* and place herself at their disposal to be made pregnant by what Heinrich Himmler, the principal protector of unmarried womanhood, coined rather matter-of-factly "conception assistants". It is for this reason that the *Lebensborn* homes were often alluded to as "stud farms". If she refused, she would be punished by the *Rasse Amt* as an enemy of the state. Otherwise, the SS were considered the "godfathers" of the illegitimate children, and the *Lebensborn* provided funds for their education. Can you imagine the SS as godfathers?

Yet, the homes were still difficult for the SS to manage because it was not easy for them to find doctors, midwives and nurses who were willing to work there, which caused a major problem when Gretchen gave birth. Meanwhile, the Red Cross refused them aid and the SS officers in charge sent letters out to the multiple Nazi organizations in order to seek their help. Children were also abducted by force from other parts of the *Östland*, from Poland, Russia, and Czechoslovakia for example, and placed in *Lebensborn* homes; their parents never having been consulted and later never informed of their children's fate. Hostels were also established in Germany, under the auspices of the *Lebensborn*, where children were tested for racial purity. Those who failed the examinations or whose ancestry was questionable for one reason or another were often returned. When Mother learned all of this, she started weeping, weeping for all those mothers who had lost their children.

I later read that beginning in 1937, even unmarried mothers could avail themselves of the title of "*Frau*". By 1939, an unmarried mother was also no longer dismissed from the civil service. The SS even came to endorse a number of financial measures to aid women who had children serving at the front, regardless of whether their children were legitimate or not. By 1943, a decision was further taken to conscript all women between the ages of seventeen and forty-five. I learned that Gretchen left Düsseldorf for the front and without hesitation lost her life for her Führer and their Reich.

In any case, our whole family concluded that Hitler had projected his amorality into his Reich, which had become stripped of all ethics. By the mid-thirties he miraculously had managed to dissolve the country of all vestiges of family life. Mother rightly believed that "the lunatic" had turned Germany into both a gigantic brothel and a stud farm.

As early as 1933, Hitler declared that "in my state, the mother is the most important citizen". This sentiment was endorsed by Goebbels, father of six, whose attitude toward women, like all Nazis, was very reactionary: "a woman's primary, rightful, and appropriate place is in the family, and the most wonderful task that she can perform is to present her country and people with children."

In 1934, Mother's Day became an official holiday, having been changed to the date of Hitler's mother's birthday. Under the Nazis, Hitler also created an "Order of the Mother", comprised of three classes; the mother of four children received a bronze cross, of six children a silver cross, of eight children or more, a gold cross and was named a "Holy Woman of the Third Reich". She had a double voice in any court as well as the right to be admitted to Hitler's presence whenever she desired. She also had priority in all government offices and was entitled to a salute from the Hitler Youth, the soldiers, the SS, and the police. Hitler was the godfather of the eighth child. Not only the SS were godfathers, but now even Hitler, himself! Now I'd heard everything. If one of these mothers needed financial assistance, she was also awarded a pension by the state. Finally, those women having ten children or more were taken care of by the state, which would also be responsible financially for the education of all their children. Their offspring were also given special land grants in the East. The mother's Honor Crosses were first awarded on Mother's Day 1939; the crosses were to be worn around their necks or pinned on their blouses.

Hitler intended, after the war, to legitimize bigamy, at least for men. The SS and the heroes of the war would be given special privileges whereby they would have the right to have a second wife, who would have the same legitimacy as the first. The authorization to have two wives would be viewed as a mark of distinction which would be remunerated by bonuses in salary.

Importantly, I was later told that women came to have many grievances in relationship to Hitler's treatment of them within the Reich. They felt that men were being educated against marriage and the family. When not spending time with another woman, men in Anglo-Saxon fashion were furthermore spending their leisure time in *Kameradschafstheime* (hostels) or in *Vereine* (clubs), while their wives were feeling isolated, with or without their children who no longer respected their parents, only the Reich.

By 1934 I was only eight, so Hitlerian psychology of mother worship escaped me. However, as an adult, I realized that the Führer's idolization of the mother, when not his own, was strictly a matter of convenience, convenience, yes convenience. In what sense? In the sense that the mother, despite all the praise bestowed upon her, was actually relegated to backstreet, like a whore, not exactly a whore, but like a second-class citizen whose sole role was childbirth. While she spent her time in labor, along with her sisters, Hitler was able to control her and the other women of the Reich, which consisted, do not forget, of fifty percent of the population... not a negligible proportion...

Long after the war ended, I took a night course on Hitler and W.W.II. Furthermore, I consumed every- and anything I could get my hands on regarding W.W.II, Germany, and particularly Hitler, himself.

> *Doctor, I was driven, do you hear me, driven to better understand why he was so evil and how the German people allowed themselves to be manipulated by him.*

I can only conclude that he besotted most of Germany. In fact, he seems to have brought the country under a diabolic spell. In any case, when you first look at his early childhood and youth, you can already see the beginnings of his illness.

Hitler's veneration of the German mother began with his idealization of his own. Until his death, he slept with her picture over his bed and carried her photo systematically in his breast pocket. Although I recognize that I, too, was always tied to my mother's apron strings, it was never to this degree. He was the classic mother's boy; the product of what is called "Jocasta mothering". He was arrogant with mother love, which makes future tyrants, like himself, or geniuses and teachers such as Michelangelo or Gandhi, respectively. Having lost her first three children, Hitler's mother, Klara, was overjoyed by her son's birth. Albeit over-nurtured and overprotected by her, the young Adolf was inversely at the mercy of a cruel and choleric father, Alois, whom he came to despise. As a young boy, he internalized his father's hostility. Consequently, consumed by self-hatred and guilt, he, in turn, projected his negative sentiments unto his younger siblings, Paula and Edmund, or even their dog, Luther, who in similar fashion were weaker and thus without defense.

Adolf's early ruthlessness was, in adulthood, manifested by his virulent anti-Semitism, the Jews his later scapegoat. By eradicating us, he furthermore attempted to render credible that he was not a Jew. Otherwise, Freud espoused that whenever a paranoid raised someone to the level of sole prosecutor, the accused was acting as a father substitute. *But this you certainly know better than myself.* Thus, in attempting to liquidate the Jews, Hitler was subconsciously attempting to destroy Alois. In the beginning of *Mein Kampf*, did he not also liken Germany to his mother and Austria to his father, whom it was necessary to annihilate? "From my earliest youth I came to the conviction which never deserted me… the protection of Germandom {the mother} presupposes the destruction of Austria {the father}". While he also spoke of Germany, the motherland, as his only bride, he accused us of sexual perversions, claiming even that we, the Jews, had sexual relations with our mothers. *Doctor, you are the shrink, not me, but you have got to admit, that, if this is not projection, I do not know what is.* Meanwhile, the only time that Adolf seemed to bond with his father was when Alois initiated his son to his passion, apiculture. The bees, not dissimilar to the Jews, were reputed for their wealth and the other bees were jealous. At six, young Adolf was already delirious when his father gassed a colony of bees and the dead were lined up to be counted as if they were in a future concentration camp. The handwriting was on the wall.

> *Doctor, Hitler was the paragon of the psychopath. He must have been the dream of every psychiatrist.*
>
> *Mr. Schwabe, Hitler was particularly obsessed by death, his personal thoughts of destruction may have been transferred to the politics of genocide. It is also possible that he assuaged his personal anxieties about death by destroying others; the genocide may also have been the consequence of his profound sentiments of remorse. It is recognized that paranoid despots seek to externalize their feelings of culpability by once again displacing them upon others, who in turn they annihilate, thus giving them the illusion of having acquired a special dispensation over death. This was certainly Hitler's case.*

Crucial also to some, and of course only some, further understanding of Hitler's motivations for our genocide is the intrinsic ambiguity over his own Jewish origins. Although, there is no completely tangible proof, there exists much supposition regarding his Jewish ancestry, whose verity inevitably terrified Germany's Führer. The theory of his Jewishness was initially exposed by his nephew, Patrick, who even wrote an article about it in the French newspaper, *Paris Soir*, in 1939. Hans Frank, the former Reichs Minister of Justice and Governor General of Poland, upon Hitler's request also researched the chancellor's heritage in depth. While awaiting his death sentence in Nuremberg Prison, Frank also confirmed in his work, *Facing the Gallows: An Interpretation of Hitler and his Age,* that the Führer's paternal grandmother had been a domestic in a Jewish household in Graz where she has been impregnated. Thus, it was probably not surprising that in his Nuremberg Race Laws of September 1935, not only were existing marriages between German citizens and Jews void, and extramarital relations between them prohibited, but Jews were forbidden to hire female Germans under forty-five for domestic service. From Hitler's creation of this last law, can we not deduce that he wanted to protect German womanhood from confronting his grandmother's fate? After the invasion of Austria in 1938, did he not also a year later even evacuate and blast Döllersheim, his father's birthplace and the site of his grandmother's grave, in order to eradicate any potential trace? For me, after all these years of query, there is absolutely not a shadow of a doubt that he was Jewish. He was a self-hating Jew, but again I am not the psychiatrist.

Furthermore, the initial qualifications of Hitler's SS[9] candidates were not only that they be very tall, but that their pedigrees be traced back to 1850 and be of pure German blood. Additionally, in 1933 in Bavaria, while addressing one of his audiences, Hitler feigned that he, himself, was of Bavarian descent. Similarly, in 1938, in the presence of leading English and German diplomats, he pretended to be of Anglo-Saxon origin. Although the Führer's possible Jewish identity remains an enigma, was it not from the beginning his Achilles heel? Otherwise, plagued by his heritage even in childhood, Adolf was reported to have had his own blood sucked by leeches, or later by the syringes of Dr. Morell. As an adult, he was also very concerned with the measurements of his head; it was a common misapprehension among Nazi racists

---

9 The SS (*Schutz-Staffel*) was established in 1925 and were Hitler's black uniformed bodyguards. Its chief, Heinrich Himmler was under the command of Ernst Röhm, the chief of the SA, the *Sturm-Abteilungen*, the brown-shirted storm troops.

that an individual's Jewish identity could be determined cranially. Thus, Hitler summoned to his Munich apartment a group of craniologists and phrenologists to examine and measure his head. He was reassured and even elated to find that his measurements were those computed from the death masks or portraits of famous leaders such as Frederick the Great, Bismarck or Napoleon. Mother was right, he was an obsessed lunatic. Can you imagine all these people running in and out of his home as if they were land surveyors?

For me, Hitler was also possessed... possessed by a diabolic mission. Heinrich von Treitschke had announced that "God had given all Germans the earth for a potential home, and this assumes that there will come a time when there will be a leader of all the world, a leader to serve as the embodiment, the incarnation, the essence of a most mysterious power which will tie the people to the invisible majesty of the nation". When at sixteen, after listening to Wagner's *Rienzi* and having climbed to the summit of the Freiberg at midnight, was it not he, Adolf Hitler, who realized that he was to be this *Volkstribun*, this leader of the German people? Hitler viewed himself as the Messiah of the Germans and alluded to a mandate which one day he would receive from the people to lead them out of servitude to freedom; he spoke of a specific mission which would be entrusted to him. Grandfather really was not wrong when he said that Hitler had delusions of grandeur and that was his downfall, not to speak of the six million European Jews he brought down with him.

However, Mr. Schwabe, you seemed fascinated by Hitler even as a child.

Yes, Doctor, you are right. Maybe because he was so diabolic, he exercised over me as so many others an hypnotic power.

When in Vienna during his early twenties, modeling himself after the Savior, Adolf even grew a long

Christ-like beard; it seemed that only the sandals were missing. *Can you believe that he even confused himself with Christ?* Afterwards, before his chancellorship, Father also saw Hitler giving a speech where he behaved like Christ, incarnated. As you remember, when Christ found the Jewish money changers in the temple, he seized his whip and forced them out. In a similar fashion, Hitler, as though bewitched in the middle of his speech, swung his whip like a madman, and with vehemence pretended also to drive all the Jews away. Not surprisingly, with time his references to the Bible and his identification with the Messiah also became increasingly frequent.

As early as childhood, Hitler also considered himself "the chosen one", given that three children had died before his birth and that his younger brother died when Adolf was only ten. As an adult, he also felt that he was under divine protection. During W.W.I when he was at the front, he heard a voice, for instance, which told him to pick up his plate and move to another part of the trench. His comrades who had remained were killed by an enemy shell. Likewise, during W.W.I when he was temporarily blinded by gas, he miraculously recovered. It was there at Pasewalk that he also had a vision similar to his earlier one at the Freiberg. The dictator saw himself once again as Germany's long awaited liberator: "When I was confined to bed, the idea came to me that I would liberate Germany." While he "liberated" Germany, he forgot to mention that he killed six million of us, European Jews, along the way. But I am still incapable of understanding how he managed to brainwash millions of seemingly civilized people. He was not the dictator of an uneducated third world country.

I must tell you that the Führer's speeches were excessively dramatic. Father took us, even Svetlana, to hear him speak one night in Munich, a couple of years before the war broke out. Mother had stayed in Riga and when she learned about our outing, she was fit to be tied. She was furious with Father for exposing us to Hitler. It was actually the first time I had heard them fight. As I listened behind the closed door of their room, I heard Mother screaming and at the top of her lungs alluding to the Führer as a "damn lunatic" and afterwards yelling at Father that he too was a "fucking Nazi". She continued that the next time that he should indulge in such a capricious venture, the whole family would end up in a concentration camp. I remember her hollering: "Concentration camps are no longer only for political dissenters, they are also for Jews, and don't forget our children are *Mischlinge*[10], and now you're a Jew too because you're married to one, me! Why the hell did you bring the children to such a spectacle?"

"You know as well as I do that watching Hitler is fascinating. It's better than any London or Broadway play. Listen, some even pay to see him. Otherwise, politics is important. They should know what is going on in the world. They should know who Hitler is. Don't you think?"

"For children, they know more than they need to know. They certainly don't need to listen to his endless tirades against the Jews. Svetlana, who is the youngest and most fragile of the tribe, you know as well as I, has not stopped having nightmares since she heard him speak. She refers to him as the 'mean uncle' who hates us, Jews. I think you might have spared a sensitive eight-year-old the Führer's venom. I still don't understand you. I wonder if someplace you're not a Nazi spy and if not, a closet Nazi. In fact, since they passed the Newspaper Editor's Law I've been questioning how they still permit you to remain a freelance journalist."

"You know perfectly well that long before Nazidom, my family and the Goebbels family have been long-standing friends."

I no longer recognized my mother; so tough and angry, she seemed to be somebody else. Furthermore, when I listened to her, I was really frightened that something might happen to all of us. What seemed all

---

10 An individual of mixed blood.

the more strange was the night that Father took us to hear Hitler, just before entering this enormous mansion, he put on a Party Badge, while reassuring us that it was always better to wear it when in the Führer's presence. But as I already said I was never a hundred percent sure where his allegiances really lay. Actually, it was not until much later that I learned he was not a Nazi.

That night we took our seats and looked up at the crystal chandelier, radiating a flood of light along the imposing marble staircase. Suddenly after a brief but deliberate interval, we heard the music of the band playing a military march. Hitler walked majestically down the aisle while his black clad SS were in reverent attendance on either side. Although I was only twelve, I was thunderstruck to finally see Hitler, Germany's demi-god. As he came down the aisle, I remember him pushing away those who tried to accost him. When he reached the platform, I immediately noticed his weak, soft face. He had large pouches under his penetrating, deeply set eyes, which were light blue with a greenish-gray tint, his lashless eyelids adding to his hypnotic power over the audience.

After another speaker had warmed up the audience for him, the Führer then began by holding up his hands and rolling his eyes toward the flickering chandelier, stating that he must thank God for giving him Germany and we must thank God for giving us Hitler. Standing very erect, rocking back and forth, as if possessed, he began his discourse as he manifested his habitual nervousness. His speech was at first slow and halting; he needed time to sense his audience. At one of his earlier meetings, Father said Hitler was initially speechless and consequently picked up the table in front of him in order to get his bearings. Father explained that Hitler was, in fact, known to speak only through association; he was always unable to speak without an awakening cue. However, that night he did gather more and more momentum until at one point much later he lost his train of thought. Then, he suddenly halted, raising his hand in order to make the horizontal form of *'Heil Hitler'*. We rose from our chairs, Svetlana shaking. Afterwards, he made an intense cry in a broken voice, bellowing "*Heil Deutschland!.. Sieg! Sieg!*" Svetlana screamed, Father went white.

As if we were participating in a trance, except for my sister, we repeated like robots the same words. Afterwards, he began to speak faster and faster with a greater degree of volume and intensity, addressing his main obsession, Jewish-Marxism. "Down with the Jews, down with the Bolsheviks", he yelled, as he fervently hit his boots with his whip. After passionately screaming out a stream of curses all against the Jews who should burn in hell, he swayed from one side to the other, we did the same, except for Svetlana who was still shuddering. He then leaned toward us and we too leaned toward him. Svetlana didn't move. The climax culminated, we rose to our feet in a frenzy and quickly fell into a state of mutual exhaustion; Hitler, drenched in perspiration, left the room. It was then, that night, even at twelve that I began to have some inkling of the hypnotic power he held over the German people.

He believed his mass meetings were liturgical rites where his audience came to belong to a greater emotional community. Many of his speeches were, in fact, orgasms of words, taken originally from his writings. Already as early as *Mein Kampf*, he also compared his audience to a woman who needed to be in submission: "Like a woman, whose mental state is governed less by considerations of abstract reason than by an indefinable emotional craving for the strength that completes her being, and who in consequence would rather yield to a strong man than dominate a weak one, so the masses love a dominator better than a supplicant and feel inwardly more satisfied with a doctrine which tolerates no other beside itself than one which grants liberal freedom. They have no idea what to do with it as a rule and even tend to feel they have been abandoned." Later, to Ernest Hanfstaengl and other informants, he frequently reiterated that the masses were feminine.

The Führer was known, too, for his asexuality and his speeches were a substitute for sex. Father said that what he did not do in the bedroom, he did in his speeches. He was repulsed apparently by sex since his childhood, when he found his father having sexual relations with his cherished mother. Looking back, I must admit I probably would also have been pretty perturbed if I'd seen Father having sex with Mother. Therefore, as an adult, Hitler also became afraid of sexual contact with women and compared it to the trauma a soldier confronts in battle. Actually, he avoided any physical contact. In 1924, for instance, at a New Year's Eve party attended by Mother and Father, a very attractive woman tried to kiss him under the mistletoe. He was in a state of astonishment and horror and remained there, shaking, biting his lips in order to control his anger. After examining his medical reports, Dr. Felix Kersten reported that he was not, however, a homosexual. Yet, according to the report, Hitler did admit to receiving sexual satisfaction from his speeches. When lacking an audience, he even confessed to satisfy himself by making masturbatory orations to the furniture.

Hitler's involvement with women was more than precarious. Of the seven women with whom he had some form of involvement, six committed suicide or made serious attempts on their lives. His thirteen-year relationship with Eva Braun ended by their brief marriage and death in the bunker. Dr. Kersten further reported that the chancellor was impotent, and their long relationship was platonic, as must have been the others. I think he was simply a closet fag.

Hitler also substituted cruelty for sex and each woman having any form of intimate involvement with him was frightened by his sadistic side. Systematically, he hurt their feelings, screamed and raged, provoking constant scenes. It seemed that Eva Braun was the only woman capable of at least tempering his outrages. Psychologically, he tortured them as if they were prisoners at his mercy. His niece, Geli Raubal, was a salient example. Aware that he was unable to love her in a normal way, Hitler locked her up in his room until she most likely killed herself; the specifics regarding her death have never been clarified.

Lastly, Hitler had a passion for films and spent many nights in his private movie room watching in a state of sadistic ecstasy the gruesome treatment of the prisoners in the camps, while Hanfstaengl, also rumored to be a closet gay, often played the piano in the background.

> *Can one not question if the concentration camps were not yet the ultimate manifestation of the Führer's sexual sublimation? But again, you're the shrink, not me.*

Hitler, who bewitched his audience like an African medicine man, or an Asiatic shaman, was also fascinated by the occult. Like most monorchids Hitler believed that he, himself, was endowed with magical powers. At the Freiberg or at Pasewalk, did he not have the vision that it was he who had been mandated to save Germany? Father told us that Hitler was actually born in the Austrian town of Braunau in medium country, which spawned famous clairvoyants such as Madame Stokhammes or William and Rudi Schneider.

Father then told us that in fortunetelling circles, throughout Germany, a new Charlemagne and a new Reich was awaited. Yet, once again, how were the German Jews to imagine that this new era was one in which they would be totally annihilated, or at best ostracized? Most had always been Germans first, and Jews second. Hadn't they proven their devotion to the Reich during W.W.I?

In any case, in the 1920s, Germany's future chancellor took oratory lessons from Herschel Steinschneider, the son of a Jewish comedian, a short swarthy Viennese who began his career in a circus swallowing swords and afterwards ran a business of clairvoyance and relationship issues in Prague, where he also had problems with the police. He was furthermore a journalist but by the early 1930's had become the most celebrated fortuneteller in Berlin. Albeit Hitler pretended to have never consulted a clairvoyant for fear of being influenced, and before the war even outlawed all forms of fortunetelling, he and many of the eminent Party members were known to make practically no decisions without consulting Steinschneider. The Führer was initially introduced to him by Hans-Heinz Ewers, also a Nazi fanatic since the start. Although the soothsayer considered that Adolf, and rightly so, resembled an unemployed hairdresser rather than a Caesar, Steinschneider was responsible for predicting his political ascension. Otherwise, Steinschneider later changed his name to Erik Jan Hanussen and dyed his hair blond, proclaiming himself a Danish aristocrat. In the past, he had dabbled in blackmail and having once written numerous pamphlets condemning clairvoyants, he then decided that it was more lucrative to join them.

In the early thirties, Hanussen gave black market performances at the Scala of Berlin almost every night. Father was fascinated by the occult and even brought Abrasha one night to the Scala, who found Hanussen completely mesmerizing. He told us that we would never find people like that in Riga... They just didn't exist. Around midnight, after finishing his hour and a half show of hypnotism and mind-reading, according to Father, he jumped into his Mercedes-Benz accompanied by his personal secretary and went to "The House of the Occult", his *hôtel particulier* which was also his headquarters on the Lietzenburger Strasse. His activities at the Scala were considered by many as a cover. Goebbels confided to Father that Hitler and many of the Nazi leaders paid astronomical amounts for their consultations. Simultaneously, he was also teaching his disciples how to develop their supernatural powers, even if only latent. He was also considered the German Rasputin; his séances of the occult terminating in orgies, where even adolescents disappeared, never to be found again.

In February 1933, Hanussen gave a reception at "The Occult Palace", which was by invitation only. All of Berlin was present. Everybody important... even Father. The clairvoyant seemed supposedly to be under the influence of some type of drug. At midnight he gave a demonstration of his extraordinary occult powers. On the ceiling the twelve signs of the zodiac were shining, while Hanussen was sitting majestically on a chair on a platform below. With a halo around his head, he fell into a trance where he predicted and described the future fire planned by the Nazis at the *Reichstag*. In spite of himself, the secret that Hitler had confided to him had been betrayed:

"The crowd, such a large crowd in the streets... An entire people cheering on the marches of our SS. Fire tearing through the night air... I see their torches aflame!... It's the flame of the German liberation, the fire rising against the servitude of old, the fire singing the great victories of the Party! Now they reach a large mansion... almost a palace! The flames pouring out the windows... spreading. A dome looks set to collapse... It's the *Reichstag* flaming in the night!"

Goebbels, Hess, and Heydrich were all present... there was no room left for error. Within instants, the Nazi medium and astrologer had fallen from grace.

Among Hanussen's clients was a man Father dreaded, Count Wolf-Heinrich von Helldorf, the decadent aristocrat who became chief of the SA in Berlin. At von Helldorf's lakeside villa situated at the Wannsee, Hanussen was also alleged to have acted as the master of ceremonies at nocturnal orgies, where he was known for having placed beautiful actresses into hypnotic trances in order to obtain for the guests their sexual favors. We asked Father if he had ever attended the orgies. He hedged, responding that he had gone there only once in order to write an article. We were not sure we really believed him. Anyway, Hanussen made the error of loaning money to Helldorf, keeping the IOUs in his wallet, considering them to be a protective talisman. Six weeks after his memorable party, he was found killed in the woods according to Goering's orders; the IOU's, not surprisingly, had disappeared.

Afterwards, Father told us that Hanussen was replaced by a Swiss astrologer called Karl Krafft, who treated the occult from a more rational and scientific viewpoint than Hitler's original guru. Originally, Hitler had Krafft leave Switzerland and set him up in a chalet near Berchtesgaden. I was later told that it was through his aid that Hitler chose the most propitious dates for entering into war, whether in 1939 or 1940. Afterwards, he managed to obtain the Führer's authorization to return to Switzerland. Yet, he continued as Hitler's astrologer, sending his predictions through reliable emissaries. One night in 1944 Saint-Blaise was attacked and the SS at that time took Krafft back to Germany where he was never seen nor heard of again.

Yet, at the time of Hitler's election, Berlin had practically become a center for the occult. The newsstands began to feature weekly magazines devoted to astrology such as *Germany's Future*, *New Germany*, or *The Seer*. In a room over a tavern on the Frischstrasse, a medium calling herself Fatima, whom Father considered the best, offered around the clock advice. While in the business section of western Berlin, fortunetellers were in abundance, receiving their clients in conventional offices and at respectable hours.

In all my later investigations, I learned that Hitler identified with the medieval hero, emperor, knight and warrior, Friedrich Barbarossa, who like Hitler was a crusader, also with the mission to destroy his enemy in the East. According to legend, Barbarossa, while slumbering, sat at a massive oak or marble table. As Germany remained in toil and disunification, Barbarossa's red beard continued to grow until it encircled the entire table. When Germany would need him most, he was expected to awaken and establish, like Hitler, an omnipotent Reich. Ironically, the Führer's "Operation Barbarossa", his invasion of Russia which began on June 22 1941, the longest day of the year, proved to be as great a fiasco as Barbarossa's failure to unify the Holy Roman Empire of the German nation.

Nevertheless, Hitler saw himself as a medieval saint unconditionally committed to his Reich, regardless of the price. He was deeply embedded in mysticism and all its trappings. For instance, he blessed banners while making a simple shovel a symbol for some mysterious rite. He believed in macabre rituals for the resurrection of dead Nazis and he also fostered midnight ceremonies at the holy Brocken Mountain. Colored pictures of him were even found in the actual silver garments of the knight of the Grail. Valhalla and knight errantry had become synonymous with his One Thousand Year Reich. The Führer saw himself as the incarnation of a combination of Barbarossa, Siegfried, and Frederick the Great. Grandfather was right on. We were all the victims of Hitler's delusions of grandeur.

Hitler's birthday, which I saw only once, was celebrated ritualistically all over Germany. Twig- and flower-garlanded photos of the Führer were placed in gilt frames and displayed in shop windows, while house fronts and apartment buildings were drenched with the black swastika overpowering the German flag. Simultaneously, an initiation rite, a midnight mass, was held to welcome the new entrants into the Party's political leadership corps at the Königsplatz in Munich. The ceremony, I have to admit, was spectacular—the searchlights, pylons, flaring torches, flags, drumbeats and the fanfare; massed choruses also acted in a magical contrast to the austerity of the Party's administrative buildings in the background.

Nazism was becoming a pseudo-religion. The housing estate in Braunschweig-Lehndorf included a Protestant church without a tower. All of the settlement was to be dominated by the tower of the *Aufbauhaus*, which was to be the local headquarters of the Nazi Party. Simultaneously, the Nazis were slandering the church. It was really outrageous. They brought false lawsuits against the monks to discredit them. They threatened children, like myself, frightening them into testifying against the clergy that they had committed sexual offenses, like sodomy. They also arrested nuns under the pretense that they were attempting to smuggle money and valuables out of the country. There were endless trials placing the children, the parents, and the church in a state of confusion and upheaval. Either in Germany or later in Latvia, even the newspapers were not spared. After Germany's occupation of Latvia, whenever I picked up a newspaper, headlines inevitably read "Seduction of very young boys in catechism class", "Salesian priest sentenced to three years of prison for perverted fornication", "Sexual transgressions of Catholic Priests", or Harassment of Children in the Lutheran Church, among the unlimited examples.

In any case, according to one ancient proverb, "no good deed goes unpunished". My last therapist explained that individuals are often most hostile to those who have aided them the most. Although this is incomprehensible to me, it was certainly Hitler's case, whether consciously or unconsciously; I believe that the Führer did not want to be indebted to us, the Jews, and consequently preferred to destroy us.

Mr. Schwabe, I think you are right on.

Don't forget that Dr. Bloch, the family doctor who had cared for his mother devotedly before her death from cancer, was Jewish; Adolf often sent him hand-painted postcards signed "Your eternally grateful patient, Adolf Hitler". His landlady in Vienna who charged him very little rent and even moved out of her own room in order to accommodate him and one of his friends was also Jewish. His Jewish godfather also generously gave him money. In Vienna he was furthermore supported by Jewish art dealers who paid a premium for his unsaleable watercolors. The most important military honor he ever received, the Iron

Cross First and Second Class for his performance during W.W.I was due to Hugo Gutmann, also a Jew; the cross was of enormous political value to him because it gave proof to his claim to be an unknown hero of the war and was thus of enormous value for his political ascension. And the Holocaust is the thanks we get.

I also understood that Hitler's hatred of the Jews was irrevocably instilled in him already as a young boy. As early as the *"Realschule"* at Linz, Adolf was first exposed to anti-Semitism, mostly as a consequence of some of his teachers. One of his schoolmates, August Kubizek, claimed that at fifteen, Hitler was already a confirmed anti-Semite. Having witnessed my cousins' virulent prejudice, this seemed completely plausible. Actually, in school he was remembered for having cursed one of his other schoolmates, and denigrating him as a "dirty Jew". Once again, I was reminded of my visit to Joachim's school in Düsseldorf. During his school years, Adolf also read religiously the local anti-Semitic paper, *Linzer Fliegende Blätter*. A Wagner admirer, he was further influenced by the musician's work, *Judaism in Music* and *Decay and Regeneration*, which was once again a denunciation of us, the Jews. Hitler however claimed that he became an anti-Semite only in 1908 when he was living in Austria and under the influence of his mentors, such as Jörg Lanz von Liebenfels and Guido von List, renowned for their racial anti-Semitism. Later, in the spring of 1920, he made a speech where he stated that "we will carry on the struggle until the last Jew is removed from the German Reich." Afterwards, *Mein Kampf*, written when he was in prison, and published in 1925—was that not another testimonial of his detestation of the Jews? He claimed that we were "the deadly enemy" and advocated, quite simply, the gassing of thousands of us, which shows he had the idea already in the back of his mind.

Yet, it was not until over two and a half years into his chancellorship in September 1935 that Hitler addressed the "Jewish question" in a major public speech and recommended acceptance of the two notorious anti-

Jewish "Nuremberg Laws"; the Reich Citizenship Law, preventing Jews from becoming citizens of the Reich and the Law for the Protection of German Blood and German Honor, already described. It was furthermore in the same year, when Hitler also threatened the annihilation of European Jewry, a threat which he repeated again in 1939 in the *Reichstag*: "If the international financiers—the Jewry of Europe and other countries—should again succeed in plunging the world into war, the result will not be the Bolshevization of the Earth and thus the victory of Jewry, but the annihilation of the Jewish race throughout Europe."

Notwithstanding the Führer's flagrant anti-Semitism, at the start he was not at first planning a mass genocide; instead, he intended to expatriate Europe's Jews. This is something I learned after the war. Even today, many people still believe that from the very beginning he intended to annihilate the Jews. *Doctor, Hitler probably became progressively the victim of his folly.* Actually, in the late 30s Hitler proposed to move the Jews to Madagascar. Poland also supported the plan, wishing to send fifteen thousand Jewish families there. Although, in 1938, Hjalmar Schacht, the president of the *Reichsbank* and later finance minister personally found the Jews much too intelligent to be expatriated,[11] he was still sent to London to discuss the resettlement.

In the 30s there were discussions of moving the Jews to Palestine. The Havana Treaty would have allowed the transfer of Jewish property from Germany to Palestine. However, the agreement was blocked by the British since they ruled Palestine as a mandate territory; emigration

---

11 In order to prove his point, he took Hitler to a Gentile chinaware shop and asked for a dozen left-handed cups, the shopkeeper explained that he only stocked right handed ones. Then they entered a Jewish store. When they made the same request, the Jewish shopkeeper complied and picking up a cup in his left hand, told his customers that he had an attractive line of left handed cups but that since the demand was so small they would have to pay a surcharge for the cost of manufacturing them.

was thus negligible. After France was occupied in 1940, there still remained a serious possibility that Madagascar would become a 'super ghetto', housing four million of us. Better that than the Holocaust! Hitler had even approved the undertaking on the 30th of June 1940, entrusting the mission to Himmler, Heydrich and Eichmann. The Nazis, at that point, were planning to recreate a Jewish ghetto like the one in Theresienstadt, where the living conditions were relatively good and the twenty thousand Jews who lived there had their own officials, policemen, currency and even stamps among other amenities; there we were spared the gas chambers, crematoriums, and forced labor. At least in the beginning. Soon, however, Theresienstadt became just a collection point, from which Jews were sent to the East and exterminated. As for Madagascar, Eichmann had even sent his assistant, Franz Rademacher, to discuss with the representatives of the multiple Jewish organizations the financial arrangements for resettlement. The Jews refused to pay what they considered to be blackmail. Simultaneously, Petain's Vichy government objected to the Jewish settlement in Madagascar and when Hitler attacked Russia, his energies had become focused on war. Retrospectively, had we compromised to Germany regarding our repatriation, we might have saved millions of Jewish lives. But this is easy to say with hindsight.

Hitler's decision to annihilate the Jews was also the outcome of Germany's military defeats in Russia, which occurred during the devastating winter of 1941-1942. This is a point on which almost all historians are for once in agreement. When the Führer became aware that the victory he had expected was no longer obtainable, he then organized the Wannsee Conference on the 20th of January 1942. He compensated for his numerous military failures and reassured himself by his forthcoming genocide of the Jewish race, which was decided during the conference.

Meanwhile, in Berlin, for instance, although the Jews comprised only five percent of the population they occupied the positions of power and prestige. Leaders in commerce, they headed the *Deutsche*, *Dresdner*, and *Darmstädter* banks, as well as the most important department stores such as *Wertheim*, *Tietz*, and *Kaufhaus Israel*. The major newspaper groups, Ullstein and Moss, also had Jewish owners. The culture of Berlin in the 1920s was almost entirely controlled by Jews, whether Max Reinhardt, Bruno Walter or Albert Einstein. One quarter of all the Nobel Prizes won by the Germans in the first half of the century were to German Jews. Was not Hitler threatened by this alien but successful force which could outshine him? Wasn't this, ultimately, another of his major motivations for destroying us? I can't think otherwise.

On the same note, the chancellor always a victim of his Napoleonic complex, perpetually surrounded himself by those to whom he could feel superior, with the exception of Albert Speer, the Reichs Minister for Armaments. His personal adjutants, Brückner and Burgdorf, as well as his three assistants, Fegelein, Günsche, and Rattenhuber, who accompanied him almost daily, were renowned for their mental deficiency. Joachim von Ribbentrop, though considered as a foreign minister by Hitler on a par with Bismarck, was if not retarded at least stupid, by Father's standards and that's even generous, since he considered Ribbentrop totally moronic. Rudolf Hess, the deputy Führer, was mentally disturbed, Martin Bormann, the Party Secretary was an alcoholic, Heinrich Hoffman, the court photographer was not only a drunkard but also a hunchback, while Robert Ley, head of the Labor Front was also an alcoholic, exacerbated by a speech defect. I can keep listing them. The list is endless. Heinrich Himmler was a neurotic hypochondriac, Julius Streicher, *Gauleiter* and editor of *Der Stürmer* was a sexual pervert, Hermann Goering, head of the *Luftwaffe* was addicted to morphine. His chauffeur, Julius Schreck was the shortest man out of thirty candidates; it was necessary, can you imagine, even to put special blocks under his seat so he would see over the steering wheel of the Führer's black bullet-proof Mercedes. Hitler kept him, however, for all his life and Schreck's death was even made a national day of mourning. One of the reasons he was so infatuated with his chauffeur was that he apparently hated to sit still. Meanwhile, Goebbels, though brilliant, had a clubfoot, Meier, his treasurer and Max Amann, his press agent, were one-armed, Amann, also dwarfish, his adjutant, Julius Schaub, limped badly and Victor Lutze, who replaced Ernst Röhm as leader of the Brown Shirts was one-eyed. In a word, Hitler's Party seemed more than anything like a one ring circus.

Hitler's sense of inferiority also led him to a state of paranoia, or at least intense mistrust. On his desk he had three pencils, one red, one green, and one black; these were used to make notes or to mark documents or letters, not by priority but as a reminder of whether he trusted or distrusted the person in question; red signified an enemy, green a friend, and black, caution. His attitude in his foreign policy reflected the same lack of trust. Hitler believed neither the United States, England, nor Russia could be relied upon, mainly because he projected his own *bad faith* upon the others. Mother was right, Hitler was undeniably a lunatic.

Otherwise, despite Hitler's ambivalence and fear of women, they still played an active role in his political career. One of his major social mentors was Elsa Bruckmann, a short, but refined former Romanian princess who was the wife of a publishing magnate. Having been the victim of smallpox as a young girl and still scarred, her apartment, Father told us, was dimly lit and she never entertained her guests before evening. She was renowned for her salon on Leopoldstrasse, which was a business residence filled with works of art and antique furniture. Here, during the 1920s she introduced Hitler to writers and thinkers as well as industrialists and aristocrats. It was actually there that Father met Count von Helldorf for the first time. Elsa also mothered Hitler, to which he was not insensitive; she gave him clothes and other accessories. Among her many gifts, she bought him an English officers' coat which for a time became his trademark. She also gave him a whip, made from hippopotamus hide and a silver knob with 'EB' engraved on it, attached to a rifle hook that acted as a dog lead. She further helped him by reading the proofs of *Mein Kampf*.

Other Munich matrons, among them Helene Bechstein, were also instrumental in his ascension, by giving Hitler money and various forms of support. Bechstein, who was supposedly very glamorous herself, bought him, for instance, a tailcoat, dinner jacket, the right clothes, even the right hats. At one point that damned rogue came to shop almost exclusively on Bond Street.

By 1932, Father claimed that Germany's hostesses provided the Nazis their necessary entrée into the salons of Berlin. Helen von Carnap, wife of the Kaiser's last chamberlain, Minna von Winterfeldt, wife of an army general, and the monarchist, Victoria von Dirksen, who received the highest nobility and members of the royal family, were among the socialites of Berlin who entertained Hitler. Victoria von Dirksen's brother attended his sister's *soirées*, always decked out in an SS uniform, while both Victoria and her daughter were adorned with dazzling swastika pins on their breasts. Actually, the swastika had become the national trademark; even dogs had them on their collars. Meanwhile, Hitler, however, aspired to eradicate the German princes, intending to have them condemned by the People's Court for espionage, high treason or sexual perversions, followed by hanging. Himmler discouraged this and convinced the Führer that the time was not opportune. In fact, by 1938, the nobility comprised twenty percent of the SS because Himmler had targeted them, believing by then it essential to incorporate many of those aristocrats who had initially opposed the Party.

Hitler, himself, one must never forget, came from very humble origins and was basically ill at ease in society. Therefore, he rather preferred the time he spent at his chalet at Berchtesgaden to the social and political mandates necessary for the success of his career. Dressed in leather pants and figured braces, walking in the Bavarian hills driving around the countryside with his adored Schreck, or receiving intimate friends such as the Goebbels at his country home, was the way he preferred to spend his time. Socially awkward, he was often ridiculed for clicking his heels when being introduced to someone. Although his Austrian manner of hand kissing was well received, he was reputed also for his nervousness, and for systematically carrying not one but two guns in his pocket. Furthermore, when he met someone for the first time, he fixed his eyes on them in a hypnotic manner and tried to overpower them. However, if the other person returned his gaze, he looked up to the ceiling. If the other individual turned his eyes away from him, he would continue to stare at him. Additionally, if the Führer felt any form of opposition, he would either change the subject or leave the room. In actuality, his sense of insecurity involved him in constant power plays of one form or another.

As much as he had hated being kissed under the mistletoe, he also abhorred dancing. Was dancing perhaps not the beginning of intimacy with the opposite sex which he had so avoided? Otherwise, although many of the German matrons had primed him for social life, he still could not avoid certain blunders. Prince Philipp von Hessen, who had married the daughter of King Victor Emmanuel of Italy was a Party member. As an example, Hitler called him, "Royal Highness", while according to party etiquette, he should have been addressed simply as "Party Comrade". His frequent teas were yet other instances when it was obvious that Adolf had not been to the manor born. Goebbels told Father that Hitler fretted like an old spinster, checking and rechecking if the preparations for his receptions were in order. He would also worry over how to dress and how to overshadow his guests as a host.

In February 1933, for instance, immediately after Hitler's election, Hindenburg had a formal dinner party where the Führer made his debut in diplomatic society. According to Father who attended, observance of prewar etiquette commenced with the habitual invitations bearing on the lower left hand corner: "Carriages 11 P.M." There was also a new regulation whereby admission was granted on several cards only; each entrance having been accompanied by a brown card. Upon arrival, each person invited had to hand the card to the attendant at the door. There was a reticence against unwanted guests, given the Nazis had fallen into the habit of arriving with two or three bodyguards, chauffeurs or orderlies. Hitler, in spite of the matrons' endless priming, remained socially awkward. He seemed to be uncomfortable in his coattails and he apparently spent his time fumbling with his handkerchief or grasping at his sword belt. When he did not completely dominate the conversation, he brooded and remained totally speechless; ironically, he was seated next to Elisabetta Cerruti, the Jewish wife of the Italian ambassador. Many were concerned that he might commence one of his anti-Semitic diatribes.

Two years later, despite his marriage to Mother, Father, being an eminent journalist, was asked by Goebbels to cover Goering's wedding. Father told us that pudgy Hermann would never have had the idea to marry the actress, Emma Sonnemann, if it had not been for Hitler; it was basically the Führer who had made her "the First Lady of the Reich".

Anyway, the Commander in Chief of the Air Forces' wedding list was supposedly a mile long and filled with *nouveau riche* expectations. His gifts were "ordered" from cities, unions, factories, businesses, and individuals of extensive means. By Goering's personal requisition, paintings and sculptures were obtained from various museums. From several large cities, he also acquired a total of twenty-eight bomber planes as well as a yacht from a major shipping company. Although he had forty-two official cars at his disposal, one of his greatest dreams was at last realized—Mercedes gave him a car, a black Mercedes, a twin to the Führer's.

Hitler arrived for the wedding with his armed bodyguards of SS driving along his wake in open black Mercedes cars. Hermann led his blond, buxom and bovine bride to the *Dom*[12] through a lane of generals, standing at attention with their sabers drawn. The wedding and reception took place with regal pomp including a ball at the opera and a private party for the high-ranking government officials. Emmy allegedly appeared at the opera decked to the hilt with a fifty thousand mark tiara, glittering over her golden braids, a modest gift from the groom; it had probably not been paid for, given that even the *Spindelwerke*[13] were hounding Goering to pay for months of late dry-cleaning bills for the white liveries of his servants.

However, Father compared the wedding party that night at the Kaiserhof to a Roman feast. Of the three hundred and thirty guests, Hitler still remained the center of attention. In fact, as one course followed another, each more sumptuous than the last, Hitler's sense of modesty seemed to be outraged by his *Reichsmarschall's* ostentation. Additionally, when the Führer rose to his feet, his chair slid from under him so violently that it knocked down a crystal floor lamp. Simultaneously, four doors, hidden in the wall panels were flung open with SS men theatrically appearing with their guns drawn. When Himmler winked, the doors closed and Hitler gave his toast.

Goering's wedding reception was only rivaled by one of his birthday celebrations two years later in 1937. Again, this party was another scene of barbaric splendor. The Goerings were the most important opera patrons after Hitler. Thus, they were able to have seats removed from the opera for the occasion. Tables were placed instead and overflowed with bouquets of carnations, lilacs and exotic orchids, while bottles of champagne burst open in the night air. Hermann was adorned with medals and

---

12 Cathedral.
13 Laundry.

decorations jangling down to his feet; those who bad-mouthed him such as Dr Hans Dräger, claimed that he wore them in summer even on his bathing suits. Once again, the lavishness was apparently out of all imaginable proportion. While normally the delivery trucks returned the unused food and drinks to the respective caterers, this time they were abandoned and subsidized by the Third Reich. The waiters and waitresses, dishwashers, footmen, hatcheck girls and musicians wandered home with cases of champagne and the remaining venison and lobsters wrapped in linen napkins with Prussian crests, since there was no paper to wrap the leftovers. In similar fashion, at an official dinner at his home, Goering also produced samples of glasses with eighteen carat-gold rims. He explained to his guests that as soon as his new order would be delivered, he would have the current sets sent to the kitchen and smashed with a hammer. Likewise, he was known to have given a dinner at his hunting lodge in the *Schorfheide* where, during the course of the meal, he was alleged, after leaving the table, to reappear dressed as an ancient German. He wore a costume consisting of a rawhide shirt and bearskin and held a spear in one of his hands. With the other, at the end of an iron chain, he dragged a pair of bisons down the middle of the room who later mated to the stupefaction of his guests. But, he amused Father.

In August 1936, Father took Abrasha and me to Berlin for the Olympic Games, an event which at one point was almost cancelled. When finally the Games did take place, they cost Germany a million marks, money well spent to render credible Hitler's blackened world image. However, Father claimed that there was an international reticence to maintain the Games because many countries were fearful of the Führer's potential treatment not only of the Jews but of the Negroes. This concern reached a climax when Jim Wango, a thirty-eight-year old wrestler who was under contract with a German trainer, won an international contest in the spring of 1935. Immediately after defeating a white fighter, Julius Streicher, publisher of the *Der Stürmer* appeared in the ring, forbidding Wango to continue in the fight, and stating his intense displeasure that a Negro was allowed to participate in competition against a white person. Soon after the fight, Wango became ill and was refused treatment in Nuremberg. By the time he arrived in Berlin, he had died of a kidney ailment. Wango's death became extremely symbolic. Hitler, according to Father, then came close to losing the 1936 Olympics. Suddenly the British, French, and Americans were very reluctant to participate in the Games, being most uncertain how their black athletes were going to be treated. By the summer of 1935, many believed that the United States should boycott the Olympics entirely; foreigners became even more leery after the anti-Semitic Nuremberg laws were passed in September of the same year. Hitler was, however, aware that the Games were essential for Nazi propaganda. Consequently, he suddenly overturned the situation by announcing that German Jews were welcome to compete and even invited famous German Jewish athletes to return. No one was duped, yet the international community was, at least, temporarily pacified, including Count Henri de Baillet-Latour, president of the Olympic Games.

The 1936 Olympic Games were only outdone by those in Greece, centuries before. In the stadium, there was room for one hundred thousand people. Apart from the grandiose Olympic bell, there was also a complex including an enormous open-air parade ground, a swimming stadium, a hockey rink and the huge *Deutschlandhalle*.

Otherwise, the yellow benches were removed from the *Tiergarten* as well as the red display cabinets containing the *Der Stürmer* newspaper, which was not even sold during the two weeks of the Games. All anti-Semitic signs disappeared from the towns and countryside; Father confided to us that Germany had previously been cluttered with posters stating the following: "JEWS NOT WELCOME; JEWS, THE ROAD TO PALESTINE DOES NOT GO THROUGH HERE!" or "NO JEWS OR ANIMALS". An official order also banned the habitual Nazi songs during this brief period.

Simultaneously, every effort was made to limit contact between the local Jews and the foreigners. The official city-plan designed for the visitors showed churches and even a mosque but avoided any indication as to the location of the synagogues.

The opening ceremony was most theatrical. The torch was lit, twenty thousand pigeons were set loose, the bands played and the people cheered incessantly. In wrestling, the German champion was the communist Werner Seelenbinder, who refused to give the "*Heil Hitler*" salute. After openly criticizing the anti-Semitism in Germany to the visiting athletes, he later, and not completely surprisingly, was found dead in a concentration camp.

We were sitting with Goebbels in seats not far from the Führer's. When he arrived the Germans always stood up, including Father, not the foreigners. Throughout the rows of spectators, we observed a sea of brown and black uniforms intermingled with sprinkles of color; the latest women's fashion being two tone jackets in bright colors. The Führer was totally immersed in the Games and behaving as temperamentally as usual. When the German, Ilse Dorfield lost the relay race to an American, Hitler jumped out of his seat, crumpled his hat in his hands in anger and afterwards sank back in his chair, shaking his head with disapproval. *Doctor, you must agree, only a mother's boy would allow himself such a luxury!* Yet, he was overtly criticized for his behavior toward the American Negroes whom he believed should never have partaken in the festivities. When the African American sprinter, Jesse Owens, carried off four gold medals in six days, in order to avoid congratulating this "flatfooted specimen", Adolf left his seat each time, returning after the next event began. Yet, when a German won a medal, the Führer applauded and shrieked in an orgiastic frenzy of joy. When ultimately the Germans won thirty-three more medals than any other country, their Führer was so proud... so proud of his Reich and his *Herrenrasse*[14]

---

14 Superior race

Meanwhile, Abrasha and I asked Father why the Führer did not want to shake hands with Jesse Owen, Father told us that this was certainly not the time to talk about it, that he would explain it to us later. We never understood why he refused to discuss the matter as he had promised but he always managed to dodge the subject. In fact, when it came to politics, he always remained most noncommittal.

At this time, did you question your father why he refused to discuss these issues?

Honestly, I didn't really ask myself the question, but my childlike instinct told me that Father was trying to hide something from us. What? I had no idea.

Anyhow, during the two weeks we spent in Berlin, we attended many of the festivities in honor of the Games. We first attended the von Ribbentrop's party and afterwards those of Goering and Goebbels. We were overwhelmed; never had we seen such luxury and extravagance.

Father told us that Joachim von Ribbentrop, often alluded to as "von Ribbensnob", was married to Annelies Henkell, the daughter of the champagne magnate; she was also among the matrons instrumental for Hitler's career in the early thirties, given that she had one of the most important political salons in Berlin. Her husband could proudly boast, but only through alliance, that he stood solidly on his two legs, "Each leg being worth a million marks". Above all reputed for his social snobbery, Joachim joined every social club imaginable, including the *Herren Club*, but was to his dismay and astonishment rejected at the most exclusive, the *Adelsclub*. Equally renowned for his pretentiousness, most of his servants were English, including his butler, Landgraf, and even his menus were in English.

This notwithstanding, when Abrasha and I arrived at their villa in Lenze-Allee in Dahlem, the most fashionable section of Berlin, we were astonished by its beauty, which to us seemed magical. Their house consisted of refined antique furniture, expensive Persian carpets and pictures signed by well known painters. The gala dinner was given outside; six hundred people attended, including most of the government and Party leadership, with the notable exceptions of Hitler and Neurath. The spectacle was one out of a fairytale, with their endless private park filled with people. There was also a swimming pool which was lit and covered with lilies, while an ox was roasted over a nearby fire.

Two days later we attended another reception, this one held by Goering at his palatial residence, where he received his guests with his usual pomp. The lawns were lit and his pool too was filled with floating lilies, while the *corps de ballet* from the Berlin Opera House danced on the lawn. Afterwards, giant screens were pulled away and behind them we discovered a Viennese fun fair. He also presented his guests with the scene of Ernest Udet looping the loop over their heads, as they turned in alarm. In addition, we witnessed a floodlit procession of white horses, donkeys and peasants, which appeared out of nowhere. Guests took rides on carousels in the especially constructed Luna Park. All the Nazis were saying that no such spectacle had existed since the time of Louis XIV.

Although only Father attended, Goering also hosted a government dinner at the State Opera House. Similar to his birthday celebration, the stage was leveled and gold tables were put out for the guests. Afterwards space was made for the opera singers and dancing.

However, the most impressive event without a doubt was given by Goebbels, a celebration with an Italianate theme for two thousand five hundred guests on Peacock Island. He had the *Wehrmacht* construct special pontoon bridges for us to gain access to the island. The path was lined with girls from various Berlin nightclubs dressed up as eighteenth century pages. Peacock Island was decorated with lights and torches. As the champagne flowed, the evening ended with a fireworks display. It was here that Barberina first danced for Frederick the Great.

Hitler, too, hosted his festivities, which were held at the Chancellery, open to the public only for the first time. Although even Father was not invited to his party of two hundred, we visited the Chancellery with him and his club-footed friend, Goebbels. I remember it being absolutely enormous, containing a thousand rooms, cinema, concert halls, many expensive murals painted from scenes of Wagner's operas, as well as an interminable hall possibly three times the length of the Hall of Mirrors at Versailles. It also included an air raid shelter with bathrooms, a movie theater, kitchen and even hospital rooms. An air raid system! Can you imagine, he was already preparing for war. However, many of the Berliners were very critical of Hitler for destroying some of the city's beautiful and majestic palaces and other historic landmarks. He replaced them with his own architecture, carrying his own indelible Nazi stamp. Hitler, to say the least, was never credited with Ludwig of Bavaria's sense of esthetics. This notwithstanding, after two years in the cutting room, the première of Leni Riefenstahl's film, *Olympia*, was held at Berlin's *UFA-Palast* cinema in celebration of the Führer's forty-ninth birthday.

During our stay in Berlin, Father also initiated us to a jazz—what the Berliners called '*yats*'—performance by Josephine Baker. She had already become a star in Paris, where she was a permanent fixture at the *Folies Bergère*, dancing the Charleston with a ring of bananas around her waist. Josephine became a major performer in the jaded nightclub world of Berlin. The Germans were fascinated by her, black and beautiful; they came quickly under her spell. Like other Negroes, to them, she was strange, primitive, exotic and even barbaric.

After a late dinner at *Horster's*, one of the city's best and most expensive restaurants, Father's friend, Max Reinhardt invited him to an apartment on the *Pariser*

Platz, where there was a party already in full swing. There, the men were in evening clothes and the women naked. Josephine, herself, almost nude, was dressed in a pink muslin apron, while another young woman was dressed up as a boy in a dinner jacket. Baker was dancing alone for hours as if she was an ancient Egyptian; Father said she could have been dancing for Solomon and Tutankhamun. The naked women lay or danced among Count Kessler and the four or five other men in dinner jackets, while Josephine and the young transvestite danced to the gramophone music. Father suddenly decided that it was probably not a good idea that we remained and took us for a coffee at the *Schiller*, apologizing to us and making us promise never to tell Mother or Svetlana about the party to which Max had inadvertently invited us. We kept our word. I later learned that Josephine had adopted some two dozen children. After what I saw, I wondered what type of mother she would be.

THE DEPARTURE OF THE *VOLKSDEUTSCHE*

After our voyage to Berlin, I must admit life in Latvia seemed flat. As much as I felt opposed to and hated the Nazis for their anti-Semitism, upon returning to Riga, I was also proud, at least for the moment, to be at least half German. Both Abrasha and I were also intoxicated by the splendor of Nazi power. *Doctor, I know had you been in my place, you would have felt the same.* As a consequence of our trip, life seemed to us to have acquired another dimension. Mother, always intuitive, could sense this change within us and seemed deeply hurt and angered by Father whom she rightly considered entirely responsible for provoking this transformation. She felt our trip to the Games, which Father deemed educational, resulted in a slap in the face to both her and her family. Since the beginning, Mother had also believed that Hitler was a lunatic. After being stopped by the SS on her last trip to the Reich and made to hand over her money and jewelry, she refused to ever return to Germany. The SS also submitted a statement for her to sign in order to allow her to cross the border:

> I am a Jewish thief and have tried to rob Germany by taking German wealth out of the country. I hereby confess that the jewels and money found on me do not belong to me and that in trying to take them out, I was eager to inflict injury on Germany. Furthermore, I promise never to try to reenter Germany.

The tension between Mother and Father grew daily; they argued relentlessly about religion and politics and it seemed that they could separate at anytime.

Otherwise, Father was displeased with Ulmanis's government, since the autonomy of German schools was revoked, the Baltic German Great Guild and Small Guild were confiscated, fourteen German business organizations were closed, two belonging to our family, German real estate activity was reduced and the German press was subject to censorship which involved him, directly. Additionally, in August 1939 Germany and the USSR signed the secret nonaggression pact, the von Ribbentrop-Molotov Pact, assigning Latvia to Russia. Von Ribbentrop and Molotov furthermore signed a second treaty at the end of October involving Germany and Latvia whereby the Baltic Germans were forced to emigrate to the Reich; their educational, cultural, and religious institutions being also liquidated. Officially, the motivation for their repatriation was twofold. It was part of the racial policy of the National Socialists on the one hand, and a means of resolving the problem of Germany's labor shortage, on the other. Mother also believed, and rightly so, that in accordance with "the lunatic's" habitual megalomania, he was probably planning a world war so he first wanted his compatriots to return home. Consequently, the Baltic Germans such as Father were required to abandon their homes and homeland with alacrity, disposing of their belongings at cut-rate prices. Between the end of 1939 and the beginning of 1940, more than fifty-one thousand Germans left Latvia on German ships. Although approximately ten thousand Baltic Germans managed to remain, no one in Father's family was among them.

The question immediately arose as to what was going to happen to us. Abrasha wanted to leave with Father, while Svetlana and I wished to stay with Mother. But for the first time in a few years, our parents finally agreed on something... that we, the children, would remain together with Mother, believing ironically that it would be safer for us. Father had heard through Goebbels that at Posen where he was to live, both the Jews and the Poles were being very poorly treated by the Germans.

Apparently, their possessions and property confiscated, they were being relocated to other regions of Poland; this was of course in great part in anticipation of the arrival of the *Volksdeutsche*[15] like Father, from either Lithuania, Latvia or Estonia. One night, when petrified by Father's departure, I decided to listen behind the closed door of my parents' room. I heard Father telling Mother that in Posen, there was also a school for torture which had been created by the Nazis in order to train the *kapos* for the concentration camps. Afterwards, maybe even worse, I heard them talking about divorce for the first time. They had decided to divorce in order that Father could regain his Aryan status. I could not help myself from telling Abrasha and Svetlana. I was so heartbroken, I had to tell someone. But we all agreed not to say anything to Mother and Father since they had not told us. We played dumb, hoping that they would change their minds.

The Overseas service of the BBC in Riga announced the *Volksdeutsche* must return to the Reich immediately. Baltic Germans with Latvian passports like Father and his family had the option to choose German nationality but only under the condition that they made an immediate decision. How could Hitler induce the German Balts, who were living a relatively comfortable life, to leave Latvia and repatriate to a Germany that seemed so uncertain, and one that many did not even know? The younger generation of the German Balts worshipped Hitler so they were very enthusiastic about the transferal. However, the older ones were very leery, fearing change and upheaval. The National Socialists left no stone unturned and even the Asylum for the Blind was closed down; consequently, the blind, accompanied by their Labradors, were ordered to Riga Harbor. Over a period of months, around forty ships arrived in the harbor and left laden with close to two thousand passengers daily. Although the Führer had promised that all the German Balts repatriated to the Polish Corridor would

---

15 The Germans living outside the Reich.

become homeowners, most left unassured. Weeping with frightened faces, they boarded the ships, along with Father, the rest of our German family members and Fräulein. As they embarked with their statutory two packages, containing eating utensils, some warm clothing and the bare necessities for the future, all the family sobbed hysterically. We did not know when we would see each other again, if at all. In the brutally cold January weather, we all huddled together, Mother trying to comfort us as best she could. It was without a doubt one of the worst days of my life.

> *You can imagine, Doctor, that with my father's departure I was absolutely forlorn as I was just an adolescent.*

A minority of Germans had lived in Latvia for close to eight centuries. This notwithstanding, the Latvians were generally overjoyed regarding their departure. Even though the Baltic Germans had made a particularly important contribution in business, at the university, and in medicine, the Latvians viewed them with hostility. Historically, for them the Baltic Germans represented oppression, subjugation and exploitation. For us Jews, by contrast, we romanticized the Germans and everything German. Although the majority of the Jewish population spoke Yiddish, the upper classes such as ourselves spoke German. Additionally for us, the Germans were *"das Volk der Dichter und Denker"*, the people of poets and philosophers. Apart from our cultural affinity for Germany, we were also linked through service to the Baltic German gentry, sometimes over a period of many generations. Additionally, Germany represented emancipation and an opening on western culture and the modern world.

Otherwise, Riga, alluded to as the "Paris of the Baltic", had a highly cosmopolitan cultural life: newspapers and theaters were in Lettish, German, Russian and Yiddish, while the city contained active Lutheran, Roman Catholic,

Russian Orthodox and Jewish religious communities. Throughout the Baltic area, religion for centuries had been the trademark of nationality. While the Latvian Jews such as ourselves were very much influenced by the German culture, the Latvians, themselves were affected by the Russian tradition. Riga still had a very vibrant night life in the Petersburg tradition: vodka, champagne, gypsies, sleighs, and *droshkies*[16] with heavily bundled coachmen awaiting their clients at the door in the snow. In actuality, Riga was a miniature of Tsarist Russia, both in mood and mentality, exuding a mixture of gaiety, nostalgia, despair and sentimentality[17]. However, since their independence in 1920, the Letts had become extremely chauvinistic and tended generally to favor anything Latvian over something foreign, even Russian. With time they had become increasingly ingrown and less international.

---

16 Horse-drawn carriages-
17 George F. Kennan, *Memoirs*, p.26.

THE RUSSIAN OCCUPATION

In June of 1940, Stalin made his major move in the Baltics when attention was focused on France's surrender to the Nazis. The Russians arrived near Riga's railroad station on June 17 as well as other key crossings and government buildings with huge military tanks. They were greeted mainly by young Latvians and Jewish communists, waving red flags and screaming with exaltation in Russian or Yiddish. Some covered the Russian tanks with flowers and jumped on the tanks, embracing the Russian tank drivers. In Riga, as well as other towns, some of the Jewish youth, among them friends of ours, even forcibly prevented members of the Latvian fascist organization, *Aizsargi,* from firing on the Russian army. We gaped in dread as some of the tanks ran over a certain number of citizens, leaving their crushed bodies on the street. With the advancement of the tanks, multitudes of cars and *droshkies* jammed Riga's streets as well as the highways throughout the country. Afterwards, some of the soldiers lined up their vehicles along the main street, while others, officers in particular, wearing squares instead of stars on their collar patches marched in short quick steps through the city, unarmed.

At first, the Russians had orders to keep to themselves and not to interfere with the Latvians; whenever they were asked any form of question, with detachment, they replied that the answer would be found in the papers. Furthermore, many of those sitting in the tanks climbed out in order to smash nearby windows and doors, carrying back armfuls of loot to their tanks. Hard liquor, strangely enough, was the major objective of these raids, which once acquired, the soldiers drank Spanish fashion; they broke off the necks of the bottle and, with huge gulps, drank the contents. Quickly inebriated, they raped almost any woman who crossed their path. Often twelve men would descend on a woman and then would proceed to molest her independently, one after another.

Later, in the diffuse summer half-light, coined the "white nights of Petersburg", we watched from a distance the soldiers in their camps, their narrow eyes and large cheekbones all the more apparent by the bonfires which lit the campsites. While some were drinking vodka which they passed to the others in clear glass bottles, others were playing harmonicas, and the remaining formed circles and took turns dancing the *kazatschok*. In their dark green uniforms or sometimes in their gray undershirts, they danced for hours, with their arms folded across their chests as they squatted and kicked their legs enthusiastically; each competing to keep his balance the longest, while the others clapped and shouted with fervor. In their drunken stupor, some of the soldiers moved away from the others, toward their women and children, only to vomit or urinate. Near the soldiers were dark trucks and jeeps lined up against the bombed buildings.

An ultimatum was immediately sent to Latvia, Lithuania, and Estonia demanding replacement of their present government by one designated in the earlier signed pacts of mutual assistance. Stalin also insisted upon free entry of unlimited troops to be stationed in strategic centers. In Latvia, a "people's government" was formed. Elections were "staged", where only the communist slate of candidates was permitted on the ballot. The communists consequently received an unlikely and overwhelming majority of close to a hundred percent of the votes. Soon after, private property was destined for destruction, confiscation or robbery and all land exceeding thirty hectares systematically was taken over by the government. The People's *Saeima*, breaking its pre-election promises, nationalized land, banks, factories, stores, and private businesses. Our press, formerly democratic had now also become a standard

Soviet one, which was very upsetting for Mother, still being a journalist.

Historically, the rulers of Russia had been very anti-Semitic, executing vicious pogroms against the Jews. Nicholas II and his court, for instance, prevented us from settling within the empire, restricting us to a form of super-ghetto in the Pale of Settlement. Additionally, in the *Ostland*, the eastern areas, the Germans had been much more human than the Tsar's gendarmes, had ever been, the Russians only surpassed by the Cossacks in their cruelty toward us. Notwithstanding Hitler's treatment of the Jews, many of us at that time, caught between Scylla and Charybdis, still deemed, like Mother, that the Russians were the lesser of two evils.

During Latvian independence, the Jews maintained an educational system which was available for preschool age through university level. There were also *yeshivot*[18], which guaranteed the continuation of a vigorous Jewish cultural life, comprising Jewish philanthropic organizations, press, libraries, publishing houses, theatres, museums and included of course some of Riga's architecturally beautiful synagogues, such as our own.

When the Russians seized power, the Jews were also subject to the same laws as the Latvians regarding the confiscation of property or the nationalization of businesses. At that time, and very upsetting to all of us, there also existed the suppression of Jewish culture and identity. The Jewish theatre, the Heder schools and the Zionist activities were forbidden, to mention only a few. Hebrew was also prohibited, being replaced by Yiddish, the language of the common man. Albeit Jewish rabbis known to condemn atheism were arrested and deported, we were still for once better treated than our Christian counterparts because we were viewed by the Bolsheviks as an ethnic minority more than as a religion.

The Communists tried to abolish religion entirely, particularly Lutheranism, the dominant faith in Latvia.

---

18 Study Centers of *Torah* and *Talmud*.

Instead the Letts were expected to worship Stalin, who had now replaced God. Huge pictures of Stalin and also Lenin decorated all the walls, accompanied by news bulletins and placards, throughout the country. By the summer of 1940, religious instruction was furthermore forbidden in the schools and instead an anti-God propaganda was initiated. The theological faculties, both the Protestant and the Roman Catholic ones at the Latvian University in Riga were closed, the observance of Sundays was not allowed, and workers were given the day off on any day of the week, except Sunday. The observance of Christian festivals was also no longer permitted.

Otherwise, during Latvian independence, by the constitution all minorities were granted equal rights, yet, in reality, even though the state granted us religious and cultural autonomy, we, as Jews, were almost always excluded from all positions in the state civil service. Consequently, many of us went into trade, industry, or freelance professions, such as Mother and Father. With the Russian takeover, even though the upper class and the wealthy, usually the Jewish propertied classes, were often targeted by the communists, other Jews became much more visible in political or public office. Jews as well as Latvians who had played an active role in the Communist Party, in the *Komsomol*, and in other peripheral groups during the underground period, some just released from prison, were appointed to key positions in the Party, in the trade unions and other organizations, particularly in Riga, since it was Latvia's capital. Particularly visible were those who had been prominent in information and journalism, especially Berkovits, who my parents mistrusted, but who unfortunately became head of the propaganda section of the Central Committee of the Latvian Communist Party. An eminent Riga physician, Dr. Joffe, in fact, our doctor, was also appointed to one of the leading positions of the People's Commissar for Health, while Blumenthal became director of the state bank. Where previously Riga's police force of four thousand consisted only of one token Jew, now significant numbers were allowed to join, many of which were part of the abhorred and dreaded secret police, including two of my cousins, I am ashamed to say.

Once again we were forced to adapt to another change. Suddenly, it seemed within a period of months that Riga had been entirely consumed by the Russians. Although for us food was scarce, never had there been so much food, hams, sausages, meat, fowls; you name it. All the restaurants were overflowing with them, Russians everywhere devouring cakes and other sweets while drinking hot chocolate with enormous amounts of whipped cream. Meanwhile, the communists were also voraciously buying up all the city, from gold and silver jewelry to fountain pens. While the women and children arrived in trainloads, looking like products of the Salvation Army or the Red Cross, they were quickly transformed, decked out in the latest fashions. Mother thought they looked like peasants. Apart from the confiscation of property, the Russians also sent surveyors to measure the outside of the houses and others to measure the inside of the rooms, since all of us, even the Latvians, were only allotted nine square feet per person. Sometimes, as many as seven or eight of us were squeezed into the same room. The booksellers and libraries were also ransacked by gangs of women. All religious works, bibles, hymn books as well as anti-communist literature and novels concerning royalty or social highlife were burned. Even fairytales and children's books, any works which did not address practical matters, shared the same destiny. Did this not echo the May 10 Nazi book burning, seven years earlier? I began to wonder who were worse, the communists or the Nazis.

Christmas was soon approaching and the merriment of the holiday festivities was in the air. I felt such nostalgia. This was the first time that we were not celebrating Christmas. Our stockings and Christmas ornaments remained packed away in the upstairs closet, with Father's Santa Claus costume that we all hoped that he would return home one day to wear. Sleigh horses covered in blue blankets promenaded joyously around Riga while the strings of bells on their harnesses could be heard clamoring in almost every nook and cranny in the city. Each of the carriage drivers was giving his horse an occasional flick of the whip so that the animals would not slacken their pace in the snow-piled streets; the women who swept the lawns in summer now used huge wooden scrapers to push and pile the snow into the gutters. Across from *Schwartz's* stood a policeman on duty between two spindly and elongated Christmas trees, while somebody had the audacity to place a stuffed reindeer in the police box at the interception of Aspazijas Boulevard and Kalku Street, where the main shopping district was located; groups of people were singing Christmas carols under the tall black lampposts. Additionally, the Russian sentries standing pompously on the street corners were now clad in bearskins right down to the toes of their *valenski*, the felt boots which peasants pulled over the rags used to bind up their feet in winter; pedestrians passed them also wearing *valenski* over their shoes in order also to ward off the freezing weather much below zero. Close by, in the square adjacent to the Russian church, young children attending a Christmas fair were running in and out of the pale blue booths with painted toys and spicy gingerbread cakes all illuminated by the twinkling lights wrapped around the individual booths; opposite them a cluster of Christmas trees were awaiting to be bought, their thin pine branches laden down by the heaviness of the snow. Further down, we passed by a series of freight cars, looking abandoned. Their unglazed windows were heavily barred and we only saw the skeleton-like hands of the prisoners grasping helplessly into the night.

In 1941, six months later, during the night of June 13-14, from midnight until the early morning hours, many Latvians and also a large number of Jews were unexpectedly rounded up. Among the lists of deportees prepared by the *NKVD* were members of the student fraternities, as well as many eminent entrepreneurs, politicians, professionals, and intelligentsia. The Russians tended to remove the bourgeois and other elements which Stalin deemed 'unreliable' or 'undesirable' from the border areas of Germany. Following the arrival of the Russians in the middle of the night, Uncle Andrejs, my mother's brother, and the rest of his family were given half an hour to pack a small suitcase each.

Afterwards, they were taken in trucks across the pontoon bridge to the *Tornkalns* Railway Station. As they crossed the bridge over the Daugava River, we were told that there was a huge traffic jam created by the empty trucks returning to collect other members of Latvia's elite. At the station, there was a long queue of freight cars having a tiny opening in the upper right corner. On both sides of the entrance, there were lines of two-tier bunks with mattresses separated only by a small space between them. There was a hole in the floor, replacing a toilet. While guarded by soldiers of the KGB holding fixed bayonets, many were teary eyed as they said their adieux to their loved ones. There was much hustle and bustle as last minute clothing and food packages were handed over to those boarding the cars. I felt for a moment as if I was reliving the anguish and uncertainty created by Father's exodus with the German Balts nearly a year earlier. Meanwhile, the Soviet authorities had further attempted to convince my aunt and uncle that their relocation would be instrumental to my cousins' future vocation. Yet, after they left from the station or others departed from the *Skirotava* marshalling yard, my family must have realized that they had been duped and they were being taken by the Russians to labor camps in Siberia and not being brought to a better life, as promised. The selection seemed quite arbitrary. However, many were part of the elite or anti-communist. About fifteen thousand were deported; well over eleven percent being Jews. Given the Jews comprised only five percent of the Latvian population, our relatively high number of deportations was indicative of the anti-Semitism of the Latvian communists in charge of preparing the deportation lists.

THE SECOND WORLD WAR

Only a week later, the password, 'Dortmund', was uttered and Hitler's Operation Barbarossa was underway. On June 22, around eleven, the Soviet Prime Minister had announced that many of Russia's military airfields and headquarters as well as ports and railway junctions in Ventspils and Liepaja had been bombed. The assault had occurred "with no declaration of war and no demands made." This message was replayed throughout the day, ending always with the same note of optimism, "The enemy will be defeated, victory will be ours!" The telephone lines were down in Liepaja; Mother could not reach Aunt Clara. Completely panicked, she sent a messenger. Mother seemed frozen in terror and kept repeating "that lunatic... that lunatic... I knew it, I always knew it... all of this is the beginning of the end." For us children, it seemed surrealistic, like losing a grandparent after a long illness.

Many people fled, mainly citizens of the USSR who had resettled in Latvia after the Baltic States had been annexed, as well as many Latvians who had supported the Soviet regime in one way or another and who were thus fearful of German retaliation. The city was quickly in a frenzy. Latvian snipers sporadically penetrated the crowds from roofs or attics, while there were traffic jams throughout the city, mostly in the direction of the station, where there was a clanking of doors, opening and closing, a rush of passengers laden with packages and bundles, all desperate to leave; porters, conductors, and policemen were omnipresent. Consequently, taxi cabs and *droshkies* were lined up in two rows in front of the station, and the station square was overflowed with buses, streetcars, taxis, *droshkies*, pushcarts, trucks and pedestrians of all ages.

Near our home, we passed by the bulletin poster on the corner, on which several mobilization orders had been placed by the Soviet authorities. There was a mandatory draft; fortunately Abrasha was only fourteen and I thirteen, thus neither of us of age for enlistment. We were also too young not to be allowed entrance at university; boys from similar bourgeois and upper class backgrounds under the Soviets were not allowed to continue their studies. We hoped with the arrival of the Germans that this might change and were both looking forward to becoming doctors like Grandfather. But given Hitler's hatred of us, we were far from sure. This was a dream that would probably never come true.

This interim period between June 22 and the arrival of the Germans on July 1st in Riga was already marked by utter devastation. Soon after the beginning of "Operation Barbarossa", a formation of about thirty German bombers hovered with their silver wings in the summer sky over Riga. We heard the muffled echoes of the first bombs exploding in the distance as well as the staccato noise of the anti-aircraft guns. None of the planes were hit; below, the sirens were wailing eerily all over the city. Over the radio, we were told repeatedly "Air Raid! Go to your shelters. Urgent. Now." When our janitor rang our bell, we raced down to the shelter with him and our neighbors. Our only consolation was that while we were with Father during the 1936 Olympics, we were obliged to seek refuge in segregated shelters in Berlin, in Riga at least for the time being we remained with the non-Jews.

While Riga was being bombarded I huddled next to Mother, frankly so happy that I no longer had to share her with Father, only with Svetlana and Abrasha, that was already more than enough. When Mother was next to me, I felt protected and believed that nothing really terrible could happen to me.

Yet, parts of Riga were quickly being destroyed. Entire streets were devastated. St. Peter's Church, with its iron rooster weather vane on the second highest tower in Europe, the Town Hall and *Schwarzhaupterhaus* were annihilated, while the English Church was badly damaged, all its stained glass windows broken, with the exception of one. Street fights took place all over the city, as bridges were being blasted. The Bavarian regiment lost a hundred soldiers as they crossed the railway bridge, which was later blown up by the Russians as were all the others. Meanwhile, several thousand Russian soldiers had retreated into one of the nearby factories where all the windows were broken and people were killed. Simultaneously, fires burned all over the city from the bombings. Firemen sped to put them out but they were often killed in the air raids. Ambulances raced nervously in attempts to aid the wounded. After a few days of shelling, Riga was without electricity and the cars stopped running. Everything was at a standstill. No more transportation, no more telephone, even the radio stopped broadcasting.

In any case, to my horrification, I learned later in the summer, that at the end of June when the Russian counter attacks had ended, a revenge massacre of Jews occurred in Latgale, an eastern province of our country, even before the arrival of the Huns. Almost simultaneously, in Daugavpils, all male Jews between sixteen and sixty were ordered to gather in the marketplace. Some were shot in the train station garden behind the jail, the rest imprisoned. Over a thousand Jews were murdered before the arrival of the German killing squads. Yet, I have to admit what frightened me the most was the atrocities in Bauska. *I hope, Doctor you can understand, please reassure me.* Not only were twenty young Jewish males like myself the first victims of a German execution squad, but worse, at least in my eyes, was the castration of fifty-six Jewish males, including ten young boys from ages eight to fifteen. I would rather have been killed than emasculated. Abrasha agreed with me. Meanwhile, the incidents provoked in the town a "festival of joy"; the Latvian women of Bauska, those little bitches, appeared throughout the town in their most glamorous attire in celebration of our loss of masculinity. I had always disliked most of the Latvians but now I really despised them.

> *After hearing these reports, I'm sure you can understand, Doctor, why until now I'm obsessed not only by food but also by my sexuality.*
>
> *Mr. Schwabe, this is to be expected, given your sense of virility was placed in danger.*

On July 1st the German troops under Lieutenant Colonel Veiss entered Riga. Over ninety-five percent of all Balts, including the Estonians and the Latvians considered the Germans at first to be their liberators. In Sunday dress with flowers in hand, the Latvians euphorically greeted the Germans. All of the houses, even our own, were decorated with the white and red Latvian flag. As the windows opened in the early morning we could hear the old Latvian anthem followed by the Horst Wessel-*Lied*. The Latvians were initially under the illusion that a new era of freedom had begun, but we feared the worst.

Armed, the first German soldiers, blond, slender, athletic and tanned arrived in their greenish gray uniforms with rolled up sleeves. They appeared in a column of motorcycles attached to buggies. In addition to the driver, every motorcycle contained two soldiers seated behind in the buggy which were filled with dust after their long night's journey. When they arrived, many were given small bouquets of flowers which were placed in their rifle barrels.

Over the radio, in his loud guttural voice, we heard the Führer, "the lunatic" on the German program. Hitler was giving national speeches about the eminent "*Deutsches Reich*", claiming as usual that the Germans were the pure Aryans and that we, the Jews, were the bane of the human race. After entering the city, Colonel Veiss himself entered the local radio station, ordering those in charge to make an announcement that there was an invitation to all Latvians to gather at Riga's Latvian Club for instructions. He emphasized that it was now necessary to destroy the "home enemy", meaning all the employees of the local Soviet government and their relatives, all anti-fascists, and above all, us Jews, regardless of our occupations. The main target was the wealthy Jews like ourselves, Jews from whom they could obviously profit the most.

While the soldiers seemed slightly surprised by their warm welcome, Latvian citizens meantime formed a large semicircle around the monument to Liberty on which was marked "For Fatherland and Freedom", covering the surrounding pavement with large bouquets of flowers. Suddenly, in the distance, we saw a group of thirty to forty Jews turning the corner of the Rainis Boulevard heading for monument square, guarded by young Latvians who were taking them to the banks of the Daugava to fill up the trenches. The crowd applauded as they passed by, crying out that at least the Jews were for once being put to good use. Abrasha turned to Mother telling her that he feared that it could be our turn next.

By the afternoon, the city was filled with violence, while the Latvians celebrated their independence from the suppression of the communists, raising from buildings or waving by hand their Latvian flags. They also expressed their abhorrence of the Jews verbally or through physical acts. They accused us systematically of being communist, and held us responsible for Soviet rule. We, the Jews were once again the scapegoat. Meanwhile, trucks appeared throughout Riga carrying small vigilante groups of ten to twelve armed Latvians wearing red and white armbands, whose mission was to kidnap the Jews, load us into trucks and take us into the woods to be killed; these mobile killing squads were soon entirely in command of the city. I began to realize that even Mother would no longer be able to defend us.

During the night, in Riga, there were additionally mass arrests, pillage and random murder of the Jews, created as much by the Latvians as by the Germans. We were particularly hated by the Latvian peasantry, and by the *Perkonkrusts*, a Latvian Fascist organization, both of whom were in complicity with the Nazis. *Kommando* Victor Arajs, himself from Latvian peasant stock, would soon head a security unit of the Latvian police and be quickly considered by us as "the butcher of Riga". His first recruits were vital, intelligent and even attractive university students and members of the Thunder Cross; this made it even worse. Otherwise, the fascist *Perkonkrusts* had been the underground source of anti-Semitism during the twenty years of independence. With the German invasion, they reflourished. Their headquarters, a black building on 19 Valdemar Street, was the center of torture and the systematic devastation of Riga's Jewish citizens. They were well known for spreading anti-Semitism through their publications. A couple of years ago, they even had the nerve to ask Father to write an anti-Semitic article. How could they imagine that in essence he would agree to attack his own family? Or we wondered at the time if they knew something we did not. Anyway, they also formed the organization for mass murders and served as a training school for the executioners. Finally, the *Perkonkrusts* were given the responsibility for arranging for the disposal of the property of the victims, much of which went to the warehouses in the *Vorburg*, a posh section of town inhabited already by the Germans.

The following evening, armed Latvian youngsters broke into our home. Fortunately, both Mother and Svetlana were out. After being hit with truncheons, we were marched in the direction of the prefecture. While en route, other young Latvians approached us, also armed. I can still hear them crying out, "Jews, Bolsheviks", as they added laughingly, "There goes Stalin's enemy". Worst yet, Mischa, probably my best friend, or so I thought, was part of the gang. I knew that Gentiles were no longer supposed to associate with Jews. However, I never expected that this could affect my relationship with my closest Latvian friend. I tried to reason with him, grabbing on to him.

"But Mischa, Mischa... I'm you're friend... your friend... I've been your friend forever." I'll never forget, he struck me across the face, shouting that I was "a damned kike". This was probably my first betrayal and possibly the worst. For the rest of my life, I've only had acquaintances. I've never made another real friend. *I hope you can empathize with me.*

Afterwards, Abrasha and I were loaded on trucks which took us to the police station on Aspasia Boulevard. There, along with others, we were ordered to stand facing the wall. When our names were called out, frozen with fear, we responded, "Yes!" or "Here!" Recalling this moment far back in time, for a few seconds I become again that petrified fourteen-year-old adolescent, wondering for the first time if I were to be shot.

In any case, the police station was terrifying. Young Jewish women, including one of our neighbors was brought in and like all the other women was stripped naked and thrown into the cellar for the purpose of orgies. We later saw her having sex with two drunken Latvian officers. Those horny bastards! Worse, they sadistically forced her husband and children to watch. Meanwhile, some of the very young Jewish girls were also known to have been raped and thrown out of one of the second story windows. I was only relieved that neither my mother nor my sister had been home when we were arrested and that my father was no longer in the country. We were also accompanied to the courtyard where old and sick people, many of them prominent citizens, had been stripped even of their underwear, bloody and beaten. White-bearded old men were forced at gunpoint to put on their *Tallith* and *Tefillin*[19] and dance and sing Soviet songs, when the police were not pulling at their beards or denigrating them by making the Jews shine their shoes or polish the pavement with their beards or toothbrushes. I was so afraid that

---

19 A *Tallith* is a prayer shawl. *Tefillins* are small boxes to be put on around head and left arm containing four important prayers.

Grandmother and Grandfather might soon be among them. Just thinking about it made me feel so helpless.

Yet, only a week or two later, two Latvian officers with revolvers in hand broke into Grandfather's office while he was with a patient, who was inevitably a Jew, given Aryans were no longer allowed to be treated by Jews and vice versa. Dressed in civilian clothes and wearing red and white armbands, coined "*Bänderdecken*", they brought Grandfather and his patient to a slum area of the city. They were brought into an empty apartment, except for a few wooden canes and empty chairs, where they were stripped naked and beaten while they leaned over the seats. This incident changed Grandfather completely. He was broken, so it seemed, by anger and humiliation. Additionally, when he returned home that evening, he found out that the German soldiers had subsequently organized what they dubbed a "requisition party" at his apartment. According to Grandmother, they stuffed their pockets with everything from food to jewelry, silver, and some family heirlooms. Grandmother had also been tied up and beaten. When we went to see them the next day, over the door we found a large sign marked BESCHLAGNAHMT, requisitioned. Grandmother was weeping, confiding to us that she and Grandfather were too old to move but that Mother should have followed her advice and left Latvia with us a year ago. I remember Mother telling her that it remained out of the question to separate her family. Already Father had been forced to leave, that was already more than enough. I could still hear her telling Mother "We've told you to leave for so long, your lives are at stake..." I kept hearing her say over and over again, "your lives are at stake, your lives are at stake." But, at first her words seemed meaningless.

Otherwise, at the beginning, at least, *SS-Brigadeführer* Police Major General Franz Walter Stahlecker, commander of the German Security Police and SD in the *Ostland*, played probably the most important role in establishing the Nazi regime in Latvia; he was simply in charge of the elimination of Latvian Jewry. Importantly, as I found out years later, Heydrich's instructions to Stahlecker and other *Einsatzgruppen* leaders were not only to murder us but at all times to cover their trail and make it appear that all the crimes had been executed only by the Latvians. Killing actions performed by the natives were even photographed and filmed by the Germans in order that the Germans could at no point be incriminated for these acts. It was also Stahlecker who sent a map of the Baltic States to Himmler, on which he had drawn small coffins with numbers indicating how many of us were left to liquidate.

Friday July 4th marked the execution of Stahlecker's orders to burn all but one of Riga's synagogues. With the help of the Arajs team, not only the synagogues in Riga but also other Jewish holy places were quickly to meet the same destiny. The Jewish cemeteries were completely ravished. In the new cemetery synagogue, for instance, in Shmerli, the Fascists set fire to the funeral parlor. Within the chapel all the caretakers and their families were also burned alive, also including the eminent Riga cantor and music professor, Mintz, with his family. Even the old cemetery, which had not been used for years, was subject to the same fate. There, several hundred Jews had been driven into the surrounding buildings and hand grenades were thrown at them through the windows. Many eminent people were killed in the carnage, including Sarah Rashin, the violin virtuoso. In any case, after a short time, there was only one remaining out of thirty synagogues in Riga, the Petaus Synagogue, which was spared because it was surrounded by tall buildings and there was a church nearby. Afterwards, the Germans used the *shul* as a livery station. What a disgrace! Why all this gratuitous hate and destruction? I kept asking myself the same question. To intimidate the Jews and propagandize anti-Semitism, that was the only answer that I could find.

When I learned that our synagogue had been burned to the ground, I felt as if I was in a boat without a paddle. I learned that one of my Jewish friends was forced by the Germans to ignite the *shul* and afterwards to go inside, himself, and be incinerated with the other five hundred Jews including our sexton, Reb Manes who used to put the Holy Scrolls on the lectern and who had been particularly supportive of me during my *Bar-Mitzvah*. With horror I learned that he had wrapped himself in his prayer shawl and was burned along with the *Torah* Scrolls. I could only say *Kaddish* for him and the others. I had no other way of expressing my infinite grief.

Additionally, when visiting Riga after the war, I learned that the bodies of the victims had not been removed from the site of the synagogue. The Russians, completely insensitive to our tragedy, merely filled in the burned out shell and placed cement over the ground, leaving the corpses buried in the cellar. They opened a public garden on the site. Some of the few remaining Jewish Latvians made arrangements for the stones of the synagogue to be made into a wall where the entrance of the *shul* existed previously and labeled it, appropriately, "The Wall of Tears".

At this time, Aunt Clara contacted Mother informing her hysterically that the situation of the Jews in Liepaja had suddenly degraded. They were forced to wear a yellow star on their left chest and back, reminiscent of the yellow patch that the Jews had also worn during the Middle Ages, again to identify them. They were also banned from public transportation, from walking along the seaside and even from walking in the parks or on the sidewalks; now the Gentiles were referring to them condescendingly as the "gutter Jews". In any case, she apparently recited to Mother a plethora of other restrictions which were equally outrageous. She also told her that they had been very foolish not to leave for the United States as Grandmother and Grandfather had advised. Uncle Clarence was also very upset because he had to place a sign outside of his jewelry shop, stating "A Jewish Business". Within a few days, he realized that this would cost him over half his clientele. Meanwhile, by the end of the month, as we had feared, all the Jews in Latvia were subject to similar restrictions.

Apart from those regulations already mentioned, Stahlecker had also ordered the stringent registration of all Jews. We were also forbidden from changing our place of residence, and from visiting a museum, a theatre, or attending a school. The order also prescribed the establishment of ghettos and the total exploitation of Jewish labor. We were additionally to be concentrated in specific districts of town where we were forbidden to leave. The Jews in the ghettos were to be given minimal food rations, and taken outside of the ghettos only for forced labor, where they would have nothing to eat or drink from sunrise to sunset.

At the same time, since the outbreak of the war, Father was constantly in touch with his friend, Joseph Goebbels, trying to organize our departure from Germany to America. However, Mother remained true to herself and refused to leave Latvia without Grandmother and Grandfather, who once again persisted that they were too old to go to "the Golden Land". Finally, the family reached some sort of compromise that we, the children, would leave and join our relatives in America and Mother would stay in Riga with our grandparents. We were to be collected by an SS sent by Goebbels himself, and brought by him to Berlin, where we were to take the boat for the United States and join members of Father's family who were already living there. Even though, according to Mother, Father felt very reassured by this solution, Mother was extremely leery, having absolutely no faith in any Nazi, no less one sent by Goebbels. She feared that instead of taking us to the dock that he would deposit us in the nearest concentration camp. In the end, no one ever came to pick us up. I think at the bottom of her heart, Mother was relieved. Communications at this point broke down with Father, so we could not find out why Goebbels' emissary never showed up. Maybe Father did not even know.

Simultaneously, during this initial period of occupation, the Germans quickly installed a German civilian administration, comprised of the SS, an elite Nazi guard, the *Gestapo*, an organization of secret police, and the *Einsatzkommandos*, special command units, in order to govern us Jews throughout Latvia. To the surprise of the Latvians, their flags disappeared across Riga's skyline, the national anthem was no longer sung and the nationalistic red and white armbands were changed to plain green ones. Latvian youths, like my former friend Mischa, given international law had not been respected, had now become part of the German army and consequently were dressed in German uniforms.

All matters regarding us Jews, were assumed by Himmler's SS organization, the SD, *Sicherheitsdienst*, Security service. Otherwise, the Latvians soon labeled the Germans "Black Power" given the SS flag was black, the SS newspaper was entitled *Das Schwarze Korps*, the black corps, the SS uniforms were also black and finally the soldiers' caps had a death's head, once again black. In the meantime, the streets were also renamed almost immediately. Brivibas (Liberty Street) became Adolf Hitler-Strasse. Another one where we lived was named Walter von Plettenberg, after the reputed leader of the Livonian Knights. Simultaneously, some streets were even labeled after next to unknown Germans, whether Carl Schirren, Karl Ernst von Baer, or Victor Hehn... You name it... After any German you can think of, as long as they were German. Meanwhile, to the chagrin of the Latvians, streets named after the Latvian epic hero Làcplèsis or the poet Jānis Rainis, among many, not surprisingly inherited German names. Concomitantly, German became the first language, followed by Latvian.

Additionally, at Riga's market place, the large iron gate leading to the market was soon closed and only the pedestrian door was open bearing a large sign, JEWS AND DOGS NOT ALLOWED IN THE MARKET; dogs had never been allowed. Jews could only buy food in a specifically designated store in the market place. Not only were the products there of poor quality but also very limited, thus many times the supply was exhausted before half the people had the possibility of being served. The Jewish rations were also far fewer than the Latvians, not to speak of the Germans. The Germans issued us ration tickets for staples, however we were completely underfed, having to survive on a few grams of bread or flour, some root vegetables, never any green vegetables or fruit, meat or dairy products... thus, the beginning of my obsession about food. *But this I have already talked to you about.* Nearby, we also passed in front of a large glass deposit with many of the Jew's belongings from furniture to fur coats. I felt like a goat that had been herded for slaughter.

Otherwise, Jews were hunted down everywhere and anywhere throughout Riga as well as the rest of the country. Signs were placed throughout the city and outside, eerily marked "JUDENREIN" or purified of Jews. Furthermore, other posters in both Latvian and German strewn throughout the city, forbade any contact between the Gentiles and the Jews. We felt completely dehumanized. Within the first month, I later learned that ten thousand Jews had been killed in Riga alone, many of which had been herded like animals to Mezapark on the suburbs of the city where they were shot by Latvian volunteers.

I later also learned that precisely during this period our death warrant was signed, and signed irrevocably. On the thirty-first of July, Goering wrote a letter on Hitler's orders to Reinhard Heydrich. I shuddered when after the war Goering's words stared me in the face: "[I] order you herewith to make all the necessary organizational, practical, and material preparations for a comprehensive solution of the Jewish question in the German area of influence in Europe". The "comprehensive solution" meant the death of seventy thousand of us Latvians, who were among the six million Jews to be exterminated.

THE RIGA GHETTO

During the early fall, we moved with my grandparents to the ghetto, located in the *Moskauer Vorstadt* (Moscow suburb), which was actually in the Latgale Suburb. The area was regarded as a slum in which mostly destitute Russians and Jews had previously lived. Additionally, it was here that Riga's Flea Market was held and where before the war, peasant women sold hand-woven linens and socks. The Moscow suburb was, in fact, built on the site of the fourteenth century Russian trading post, which had been the place where, ironically, over two hundred years ago, runaway serfs had fled, given that after two years they automatically earned their freedom. We now, the Jews, had inversely become the kidnapped slaves in their place.

This notwithstanding, as we Jews had been forced to turn in our cars and were allowed no form of public transportation or permitted to walk on the sidewalks, we laboriously transported to the ghetto by hand, in a wheelbarrow, or by horse and wagon, the limited clothing and household goods authorized us; anything of value, of course, having been ordered to be left behind. All of us felt as if we were part of a funeral procession... and, little did we know, so we were.

Otherwise, the fence around the ghetto was guarded by the Latvian police under Arajs, who were among the most trustworthy of the German collaborators. The ghetto gate was at the corner of Sadovnikova and Lacplesa Street, where a sign hung above it announcing that "Jews provided for a fee. This includes *Wehrmacht* jobs". Later, a second gate was built to ensure even greater security. If any Jew attempted to escape, ten others beside himself were killed as punishment. Even the Daugava River was infested with traps designed to catch any Jews who attempted to escape. In order to motivate the non-Jews, rewards for our capture were known to be very sizeable.

The Riga Ghetto itself, along with those of Daugavpils and Liepaja were the largest ones established in Latvia. The Riga Ghetto, set over twelve blocks and surrounded by barbed wire two and a half meters high, held the most people, housing initially close to thirty three thousand. Given that according to the ghetto rules we were allowed only thirteen square feet per person, the fact that we managed to find an apartment on 35 Ludzas Street consisting of a bedroom, kitchen, living room, toilet stool as well as a sink in the kitchen was close to a miracle. Despite the fact that on the downside there was no bath, the wooden floors were badly damaged, and the house really needed painting, and even though by November we had to burn even the furniture to brave the fiercely cold winter, we were still fortunate, at least in relative terms, given many of our friends had been confined with their families to one room.

Furthermore, soon after our arrival, German soldiers came to our homes in order to collect all of our remaining money and jewelry. I remember well feeling so terrified when the soldiers, drunk, arrived at our apartment. Smelling also of tobacco and gun oil, they shouted in their harsh guttural voices, telling us to place all our valuables on the kitchen table. At that time, poor little Svetlana was thrown against the wall and struck violently across the face by two of those monstrous German bullies. Admittedly, it was one of the moments in my life when I felt the most torn. Reason, for the moment, dominated, so I didn't protect her. I could do nothing, nothing... Somewhere, I have to admit, I hated myself for this... still hate myself even though I realized it was for the best. But if even today should I ever come across one of them, I would probably kill him... kill him, for touching my little sister.

They also threatened that should we retain any of our cash or valuables, a hundred Jews along with ourselves would be murdered. Mother believed that the authorities were exaggerating and trying mainly to intimidate us so she only gave them a small portion of what we had left; the rest remained hidden in the yard or under the wooden flooring. Even though we were fortunately never caught, others were and many Jews were actually sacrificed. Additionally, the soldiers broke into our apartment, as they did with many of the others, when no one was home and stole whatever else took their fantasy.

Each morning Abrasha, myself, and Mother lined up on Prager Strasse in columns waiting to be collected for work. From where we stood, we could see Tin Square, the ghetto's main square where the gallows were also located and where more often than not one of our fellow Jews had fallen out of grace and would be hanging, usually for trading, "organizing"[20] something at work, or for attempting to escape. In addition, no one left or returned to the ghetto unaccompanied. Despite the cold, women no longer being allowed to wear hats, I watched mother, a black turban around her head nervously awaiting her turn to depart. She had been assigned a job as a housekeeper in one of the apartments occupied by a German SS. I only worried he would take a fancy to her. On the other hand, I had to be practical and realized even then that it was in this type of job that food could be the most easily procured, certainly not in the electrical plant assigned to Abrasha and myself, where we were not even given either a crust of bread or a drop of water all day. In fact, Mother had sewn inside pockets in her clothes just for this purpose and returned home not only with food but even jewelry, given the soldier's drawers were brimming over with valuables, whether rings, bracelets, necklaces, in fact almost all types of jewelry, not to speak of his closets packed with fur coats, stolen, of course, also from the Jews. He, like the other German SS,

---

20 Trading, stealing, exchanging and any kind of illegal action.

saved the best for himself and sent the rest to the Reich. This had quickly become a ritual! However, the problem arose when in the evenings Mother returned from work, where at random we were stripped naked and where particularly the women were afterwards frisked by the guards, in particular the good looking ones like my mother. If we were caught with food, the person was either shot, placed in confinement or punished with blows.

In the middle of November, Mother returned home completely battered, explaining to us that she had, in fact, been frisked at the gate, that they had found food in her pockets, and that she would no longer be returning to work for the German. It was only in her memoirs written years after the war that I learned that my fear regarding the SS was well founded. Not only had he been attracted to Mother but, intoxicated, had raped her and beaten her up. Mother... Mother... dear Mother, you loved us so much, you wanted to protect us. You were right, how right you were. It is your love that gave us strength. It's why I am still here today—because of you. Anyway, there is not a shrink alive who would berate the power of mother love.

Simultaneously, there were many suicides, particularly when people first arrived. Mainly an overdose of sleeping pills. Others jumped out of windows, slashed their wrists, one of our neighbors even sat outside with his whole family and froze to death. One of our parents' dearest friends, Chana Mersel, poisoned her two daughters and four-month-old nephew, before committing suicide herself. As they had no remaining family, we buried them in the Jewish cemetery, located in the middle of the ghetto. Children were also taken out of the ghetto in sacks with garbage or other loads. Sometimes they were sent out in carts designed to transport horses or were thrown over the barbed-wire fence to waiting Latvians, many people obviously anticipating the worse.

The older Jews were also very vulnerable, and when Grandfather was working at the ghetto's hospital, *Linas*

Hatzedek, Grandmother visited the old age home in an attempt to give moral support to some of her friends who were alone. The home consisted of one large hall with beds jammed impersonally side by side along both long walls. It was also poorly ventilated and the air was stale and oppressive, making it almost impossible to breathe. This notwithstanding, her friends and the others tried to maintain their courage in front of an overwhelming sense of solitude and adversity.

The first phase of our carnage was alluded to, in vernacular terms, as the Stahlecker phase and lasted until the end of October when all of us Jews, had been herded into the ghetto and the city was "JUDENREIN"; not even a token Jew was left. During this period, all of the Jews in the rural areas were executed. At this time, Jews were also murdered in the cities, whether Riga, Jelgava, Liepaja or Daugavpils, but we were not yet completely annihilated as we were in small towns such as Preili, Varaklani, and Gostini, where whole populations were mercilessly exterminated. In Riga, as in other large cities, the creation of the ghettos actually delayed the total extinction of the Jews. The second and last period was alluded to as the Jeckeln phase, after Friedrich Jeckeln, Higher SS and Police Leader North. Friedrich Jeckeln had been in charge of killing the Jews in Ukraine during the summer and fall, until November when he was sent to Riga by Himmler himself, with orders to empty the ghettos on the Baltic. Notorious as one of Himmler's confidants and minions, Jeckeln followed out his orders to perfection. He chose the Rumbula Forest, a pine-covered hillock, ten kilometers to the southeast of Riga near the Rumbula Station, where within a month, Jeckeln had been responsible for the execution of a total of about twenty-eight thousand of us, Riga Jews, on November 30th and December 8th. With the exception of Babi Yar, The Big Action, the Jeckeln Action and the Rumbula Action, in Latvian simply alluded to as Rumbula, was historically the largest two day atrocity for the Jews, prior to the operation of the death camps.

Just speaking about it, even thinking about it gives me nightmares. On November 27th we were informed that a large part of the population, those specifically living on the east side of the ghetto, would be resettled and we were told to assemble in front of our living quarters within the next two days with a maximum of twenty-five kilos of clothing, food and personal items. We were all terrified, as rumors had been very recently spread that massive graves the size of two square blocks were being dug by the Russian prisoners of war in the Rumbula Forest at the very end of Maskavas Street. Were they not for us? The next day, all able-bodied men over sixteen were also ordered to assemble at the gate. Abrasha and I feigned to be a couple of years older than we actually were, figuring that if anyone were to be saved it would be men such as ourselves; as the Germans direly needed work force. On the other hand, since our arrival, many young men, also slightly older than ourselves, had been randomly chosen as hostages and imprisoned in Riga's jail. In retribution for any partisan activity, we were told that ten of these men were usually selected from the prison, again haphazardly, and taken to the nearby forest or cemetery and murdered. Would we too become hostages? This was the risk.

Concurrently, on the 29th, Mother and the other women were ordered not to go to work and to remain in the ghetto. A bulletin proclaimed that women with sewing and tailoring abilities should report to the *Judenrat*, the Jewish Council, About three hundred women showed up, including Mother, Grandmother, and Svetlana who was obviously too young, but like ourselves pretended to be older. They too made the same calculation as Abrasha and myself, simply, that this was probably the only way they might be spared. Once again, only because they were needed by the Nazis for their war effort. Concomitantly, Grandfather remained fatalistically in the hospital attending to his patients, waiting for everything to blow over or not. Like others of his generation, given he had lived through one war against the Germans, he figured he would survive another. That same evening the women were taken to the prison near *Brasla* Station and a couple of days later joined by two hundred others. The majority remained incarcerated for about two weeks, and one night, in mid December, were moved into two houses in the ghetto on the corner of Ludzas and Lieknas Streets, which came to be known as the Women's ghetto. Meanwhile, Abrasha, myself and the other able-bodied men were relocated to the newly created work camp, referred to as the Little Ghetto, located across from the Women's ghetto consisting of a group of small shabby houses, without suitable accommodation for the remaining four thousand Jewish men.

Although our family had been spared the first *Aktion*, we were part of a small minority. Within the next few days, roughly a thousand Jews had been killed in the ghetto alone as well as fifteen thousand in Rumbula, including a transport from Berlin of another thousand people. On the night of November 29th, the pogrom began, as detachments of drunken Latvian and German guards led by Latvian SS, Herbert Cukurs and German SS led by *Sturmbannführer* Dr. Rudolf Lange swarmed into the streets and terrorized the Jews. Apart from administering merciless beatings and shootings, they took sadistic pleasure in tearing babies from their mother's arms, throwing them in the air and using them as target practice. If not, they gratified themselves by throwing the infants against the posts of houses so their skulls would split open. Simultaneously, people were ordered to dress quickly and form columns of five, and then most were chased and flogged with rubber truncheons and whips in the direction of Rumbula Forest. Others, mainly women, children, and the sick and the elderly, were driven to the forest in ominous blue buses not to retard the men and able-bodied.

Such was the case of Svetlana's best friend, a gypsy girl a bit younger than her called Rebecca. She was sent to the Jewish ghetto because when her parents had recently been murdered by the Russians, a kind Jewish spinster, having no family of her own, took pity and adopted her. Though her foster mother was shot in the forest, Rebecca, not shortly after reaching Rumbula, cleverly and instinctively threw herself in the pile of clothes which the Jews had been forced to take off upon arrival. She told us later when the truck she was in had stopped, all the passengers got off, being hit again relentlessly with rubber truncheons, while the German soldiers screamed *Heraus!, Heraus!* (Out! Out!) as they also whiplashed their victims. When the Jews got outside the truck, they found themselves in front of a wall of armed soldiers who were temporarily creating a barrier on the road near the forest. Rebecca told us that further on, other "mean, angry uncles"—she and Svetlana even spoke alike—stood in a row very close by each other and nearby them there was a wooden box attended by a soldier holding a club, where they were collecting any remaining valuables. Not far from the box was a heap of furs, coats and padded jackets, next to a second one piled with shoes and other footgear. According to Rebecca there were six huge trenches with machine gunners who stood at each corner of the graves, shooting at their naked victims. Screams were heard throughout the area, many even precipitating ahead in order to advance their turn in attempts to avoid an endless wait on the freezing winter day. When the Latvian and German soldiers only wounded the Jews with their machine guns, they finished them off with a revolver. We later learned from some Latvian acquaintances that Jeckeln had a special technique for which he had become reputed called "*Sardinenpackung*". After the killing of a Jew who had already been shot and had fallen into the grave, a second Jew was placed face down between the legs of the first and shot from above. In any case, the shooting began at 8:15 AM and only ended at 7:45 PM the same day. As not everyone had been killed, it continued on into the next day. Rebecca was found two days later when the Germans were sorting out the clothes. She explained that she was a gypsy and not a Jew. At the end of the pogrom she was brought back to the ghetto miraculously by one of the German guards who weepingly told her that he had a daughter of her age and that he had been forced by the Nazis into becoming a *sonderkommando*[21] for him a murderer. He also told her that the gypsies were as sought after as the Jews so it was better to pretend she was Latvian. Rebecca was returned to the ghetto after the second carnage, accompanied by her "good uncle", carrying around the customary aluminum metal marked *Ohne Eltern*, without parents.

Before the second *Aktion*, in order to reassure many friends and family, numerous ghetto members received forged letters from those who had departed in the first *Aktion*, speaking of their well being. One of these letters, received by a friend of mine, read as follows:

Dearest Son,
Just a word in case you should worry about us following last week's tragedy. On the contrary, we have been resettled very happily a few hours outside of Riga. Where we are, living conditions are more than adequate. We are expecting you very shortly.

Your Beloved Mother.

Both the Latvians and the Germans really tried to take us for fools. After the first *Aktion*, the ghetto remained in a state of total disarray. Corpses were strewn along the street, while frozen rivulets of blood lay along the sidewalks, as well as upon the steps and walls of many of the houses. Broken furniture, suitcases, baby carriages, toys, everything you can think of, were cluttered aimlessly all over the ghetto. Some of the young men from the Small Ghetto were pulling the dead bodies on sleds to the old cemetery, where they were incinerated and their ashes

---

21 A soldier who was part of the killing squad.

were buried. Corpses were also buried directly, but this created more problems, given the Orthodox Jewish men and women were not allowed to be inhumed together. Today, the Jewish cemetery has become a beautified park without any indication that the remains of many Jewish victims are there. The Latvians and the Russians obviously chose to forget us. Amazingly, in this surrealistic world, until the very end, all of these illustrious Jews, including, of course, Grandfather, were still addressed even by the Germans as *Herr Doktor* or *Professor*. Another irony.

A week later the second *Aktion* took place. This time roughly ten thousand were shot at Rumbula and another thousand murdered in the ghetto itself, including Simon Dubnow, the famous Jewish historian who wrote a ten volume children's history of the Jews in Yiddish. His last words were "*Schreibt, Yidden, Schreibt*", ("Write, Jews, Write"). And so we have. In the meantime, the second *Aktion* was basically a repeat performance of the first, except we lost our Grandfather, our beloved Scheima. Since the start, there had always been more doctors than drugs and medicine. That was the initial problem. Now that we were roughly twenty-eight thousand Jews less, the Germans decided that many of the doctors were superfluous. Grandfather, and many others were loaded into two trucks and taken into Rumbula Forest to be murdered. We learned later from one of the Latvian drivers who was sobbing hysterically, comatose from disgust and grief, that the doctors had taken poison, and for some reason still unknown to many of us, the Germans changed their mind, but by then it was too late, given all the doctors had poisoned themselves. Although they were all taken to the Small Ghetto to have their stomachs pumped, none survived, including Grandfather whom Abrasha and I dragged to the cemetery by sled, accompanied by our other family members. There again the family said *kaddish*. Yet, it was then that I really began to question whether God existed and if so was He, himself, if not the Devil, at least evil. In any case, if he did exist, he could certainly not be innocent. Hadn't even the court in Elie Wiesel's *Night* proven him guilty?

I also asked myself what made our executioners kill. What motivated them? Some, I concluded were gratuitously sadistic and any scapegoat was the right one. During Rumbula, the head of one of the firing squads, for instance, forced several hundred Jews of all ages to strip naked and to run through a field into a wood and then mowed them down with a machine gun. He also photographed the proceedings, allegedly with malicious delight.

Generally, however, there was a marked difference between the Latvians and the Germans in their attitudes regarding the shootings. Historically, the Latvians had been reputed for their nerves of steel. During the period of the Tzar, they were therefore always chosen to be the executioners, never the Estonians or the Lithuanians. Otherwise, as you know, both the Germans and the Latvians had been cleverly brainwashed that we, the Jews, were synonymous with the Bolsheviks. Thus, particularly the Latvians, who had been, in one significant way or another, Stalin's victims, were more impelled to join the execution squads. Thinking about it now, it almost makes me want to forgive Mischa. Today I realize, he must have wanted to avenge his parents' deportation to Siberia with the others in June of 1940. Unlike the Latvians, when the Germans became executioners, it was usually a form of punishment. The young Germans, like my detested cousins, entered the military with the same idealism they had earlier entered the Hitler youth. Yet, to their surprise, the moment they made the most minor mistake such as falling asleep on sentry duty, after being court-martialed, they were told they could escape punishment only by volunteering for special *Kommandos*. They were afterwards threatened with death if they refused to participate in mass murder, such was apparently the case of Rebecca's "nice uncle". In reality, however, the soldiers who were unwilling to partake in the killings found themselves with a promotion blocked or given a punishment transfer and not shot to death as threatened.

Otherwise, as we later learned from Rebecca's "nice uncle", the shooting squads underwent three-week training. During this period, he and those in his course were often encouraged to shoot simultaneously with other soldiers, in order, he imagined, to lessen each person's sense of guilt and responsibility. He also confided to us that almost systematically the soldiers were taken to Rumbula in trucks, and upon arrival found another truck filled with *Degvins*, the local vodka, so that they could drink themselves into oblivion in order to make their task less stressful. Yet, the men in the firing squads, especially the Germans, suffered from fits of hysterical crying, nervous breakdowns or temporary impotence. He recounted to us that one soldier during the first pogrom even underwent a form of mental derangement whereby he shot at random everybody and anybody around him. A number of the members of the killing squads were also committed to mental asylums. Himmler also established a convalescent home outside of Berlin, whereby many of the soldiers such as Rebecca's "nice uncle" could recover.

In any case, gas chambers in Riga were not even necessary due to the efficiency of *Einsatzgruppe A*, the mobile killing squads. However, in early 1942, Himmler ordered that the elderly and the women and children be killed by poisonous gas throughout the Reich. During that year, two gas vans were brought to Riga for that purpose. They were manufactured by *Saurer Werke* in Austria and each could kill fifteen to twenty-five people at one time. When the vans were fully loaded and began to move, carbon monoxide exhaust was fed into the rear. Anyhow, the SS found them very frustrating because they always broke down, having some form of mechanical difficulty. I later also read that General Ohlendorf, when questioned at his trial in Nuremberg, also alluded to the fact that the burial of those gassed in this way was particularly unbearable, given the stench of the dead corpses.

In any case, when I returned to Riga so many years after the war, I found the burial grounds in Rumbula to have the appearance of a peaceful, shaded park within a forest of pine trees that were so high that they seemed to be touching the sky. The trees were only separated by paths and raised mounds, indicating the site of the original graves. When I first entered the forest, I was shocked to find a small slab with a hammer and sickle in the right-hand corner inscribed in Latvian. Russian, and Yiddish: "To the Victims of Fascism, 1941-1944". Simultaneously, among the several commemorative stones, the oldest one states that fifty thousand victims of German fascism, political prisoners and prisoners of war are buried there; in actuality, only Jews are buried in Rumbula as well as Bikernieku forests. Our few remaining friends and acquaintances in Riga allude to this with irony as "The Aryan Compromise".

When I went to the annual memorial service in 1972, many of the young Jews who were attending outwardly condemned the Russians and their veiled anti-Semitism. Even though the KGB could not easily forbid the service, they did everything in their power to disrupt it. When not photographing, for whatever reason, the participants played loud abrasive music which was heard through the speakers in the trees. I was appalled to see so little respect for our dead.

Ironically, after the carnage was over, there was a heated exchange of mail between the German armed forces in Riga and the SS and the SD in Germany, where the former complained bitterly that the two *Aktions* had severely cut into Riga's labor force. Yet, if nothing else, they at least helped prolong the lives of the thousands of Jewish deportees from the Reich, whether from Czechoslovakia, Austria, or Germany. The Germans in general considered the Latvians, a *Bauernvolk*, a lower race, finding us uncultured and unreliable, while we in turn viewed them as materialistic and soulless. Yet, more importantly, many of us Latvian Jews, myself included, questioned whether our families had not been murdered to make room for the newcomers. Also we could not help but be resentful that they unlike ourselves, were still blessed with their families alive, at least for the moment. Regardless of our feelings of antagonism, we were still helpful to the Reich Jews, smuggling milk and food into the ghetto for their children at our own risk. Knowing Riga and speaking Latvian, it was also easier for us to barter and afterwards to bring into the ghetto whatever necessities were required.

Otherwise, the Latvian ghetto was an all male society, most of the Latvian women having been killed in the pogroms, while the German ghetto was the reverse, since the majority of men in the transports from the Reich had been sent for work to Camp Salaspils. On the whole, however, the Latvian Jews were a much greater asset to the workforce because many had been craftsmen and skilled workers, unlike the others who were part of the former middle class population of the German Jews in business and the liberal professions; therefore, they could only be used for unskilled labor. Anyway, while we the Latvian Jews continued to wear the yellow Star of David on the back and front of our clothes, the German Jews wore the yellow Star of David on their chests with the word *Jude* in German letters, which seemed reminiscent of Hebrew script. In addition, the German ghetto was comprised of ten groups, which were classified by city of origin, Cologne, Kassel, Düsseldorf, Bielefeld, Hanover, Prague, Berlin, Leipzig, Vienna, and Dortmund.

Both Abrasha and I were members of *Betar*, a right-wing revisionist Zionist group, and we soon arranged for Friday night meetings with the members of the same organization in the German ghetto. We met in their ghetto, where Betar songs were sung and speeches made in a room set aside in a house close by to the hospital. It was here I met Zenta, my first girlfriend. She was a beautiful blue-eyed, blond Aryan-looking girl of thirteen. Previously, Zenta had come from a middle class family of lawyers and had been separated from them during a selection in Vienna in January of 1942. Zenta had been sent to the left and the remaining members of her family to the right. She feared that she had been one of the children slotted for death. But she really did not know. I could only try and reassure her. Meanwhile, her parents and three older sisters, she imagined, were still in Vienna. But with all the selections and transports, she could not be sure. Clutching at my hand, she told me about her trip from Vienna to Riga where, separated from her family, she was brought to the ghetto, like the other Austrian Jews, in third class railway cars since fortunately for her and the others, cattle cars had not yet been used for transport. On the second day, the train had suddenly stopped in a snow covered open field for refueling near a station. The doors opened and they were permitted to get water. She and the others saw many trains passing in both directions. Not far from where they stopped, Zenta also saw one train filled with German soldiers and Red Cross attendants. She imagined they were suffering either from frostbite or from other war injuries. The enemy had also made a campsite with a huge bonfire and were drunkenly singing patriotic songs. As Zenta and the other Viennese continued, she, at one point, fainted from fear. When they arrived at *Skirotava* Station, they were welcomed by *Obersturmbannführer* Rudolf Lange, head of the *Einsatzgruppe A,* and one of the major participants in the two earlier pogroms. His notoriety had become so great that in January 1942, he was even one of the fourteen high German officials to be invited by Reinhard Heydrich to attend the Wannsee Conference in order to finalize the ultimate plans for the Final Solution.

In any case, Zenta told me that when she was rushed out of the railroad car with the others, they were greeted cordially by Lange, a tall, dark haired man in a fur collared uniform. With hypocrisy, he addressed them as "Ladies and Gentlemen", giving them the choice of the spooky blue buses or a six-kilometer walk on foot in the forty-degree-below-zero weather. Zenta fortunately chose to walk, but told me that once on the road, Lange seemed to have a personality change, suddenly insulting them and treating them with contempt until they reached the ghetto. Once in the ghetto, for months she searched for the others who had left on those awesome blue buses, but as none ever returned, she feared the inevitable.

Like Svetlana, she was very artistic but while my sister was especially adept at dancing, Zenta was a gifted painter, particularly of watercolors. When I first noticed her, she was lighting the candles for the *Oneg Shabbat*, the Friday night celebration of the Sabbath. As she lit one candle after another, I remember her face glowing mystically in the light. Later, we danced the *hora* until the early morning hours. Her body rubbing next to mine, I felt sooner or later she would be my first woman. As the months went by, we spent as much time as possible with each other, usually on Sundays when I did not work. I would get the necessary pass into the German Ghetto, where we would spend the day endlessly talking... oh, we talked so much, almost always about our past or our future, rarely about the present. We often also listened to a Sunday afternoon concert. In fact, I later learned from the Polish deportees that the Warsaw ghetto, which was much larger than ours, had five theatres and musical performances at least once a week. However, they, unlike ourselves, were forbidden to play German music and the Jewish musicians in Warsaw concentrated on Mendelssohn, Meyerbeer, Halevy, Offenbach and a litany of Yiddish and Hebrew folk songs. Our programs fortunately consisted instead of Brahms, Haydn, Mozart and Beethoven, all of the music on which I had been weaned by my parents and grandparents. Actually, whenever I attended these concerts, I felt as if I was eating a *madeleine*[22]. Happily, I escaped reality, returning to the most precious moments of my boyhood, particularly those summer days at Jurmala with all my family.

---

22 In Marcel Proust's *Remembrance of Things Past*, the madeleine was a small cake that when eaten brought back the author's childhood memories.

We also attended plays together which were also held exclusively in the German ghetto. Like some of the concerts, the performances always took place in the largest auditorium which was in the *Gewerbebetrieb*. It was a factory-like building where some of the women, by this point even my grandmother, along with other of the older women, sorted out the clothes left behind by the dead. Inevitably, each time we attended one of the performances, we could not help but be reminded of all the recent atrocities. Anyhow, each play lasted a few weeks and performances were held on Saturday and Sunday evenings. Albeit tickets could be reserved, most were obtained on a "first come, first served" basis. Our despised *Kommandant* Krause was ironically one of the ghetto's major patrons; the first three rows consisting of chairs were reserved for him, the rest of the SS, and the ghetto elite. The other rows behind were comprised of long benches and allotted to us, mere mortals. Excerpts from Zweig's *Jeremias* or Goethe's *Faust*, among many others, were performed. Whenever we saw Goethe's *Faust*, I wondered if Hitler and the Nazis had not also made their pact with the devil. Furthermore, variety shows were held, and from time to time Svetlana partook in one of the Sunday performances. Watching her perform on the stage, with its luxurious dark red velvet curtain reminded me of her earlier performances. Yet, when in Riga she danced, it seemed so natural, while here watching her perform in this ominous building gave me the sensation of something perverse. Were Svetlana and the others not dancing a death dance?

In the meantime, in this nightmarish land of the ghetto, apart from concerts and plays, sports were probably the most significant hobby and distraction of the inmates. Initially, the Latvian ghetto was especially known for its musicians such as the concert violinist, Percy Brandt. Krause's love of music further propelled him to rummage through the baggage of the diverse transports, searching for various and sundry instruments which could be used for the Sunday afternoon or evening concerts in the German ghetto. This notwithstanding, soccer soon became a focus of equal importance. At first, the Latvian Jewish police were reputed for their soccer team; their claim to fame being Schulmann, a former prizefighter and afterwards their goalie. The matches were held ironically on Tin Square, where the team was later murdered. By late spring of 1942, several other teams in the ghetto had been formed whether Prague, Dortmund, Berlin, Hanover or Vienna. The ghetto police of both the Latvian and German ghetto competed. Several hundred spectators watched the matches. It was really a happening. The Sunday matches were as popular as the baseball matches at Yankee Stadium. The Berlin, Hanover and Vienna teams wore white pants and shirts, the Dortmund, if my memory doesn't fail me, black and white. These matches lasted until the ghetto was liquidated in November of 1943, despite the fact that there was always a gap here and there, given a player was sometimes sent to an *Aussenkommando*[23], or shot or hung. It seemed so strange to be living a life seemingly normal on the one hand and on the other to be walking each day, simultaneously, a thin line between life and death.

Concurrently, Günther Fleischel, in order to mark the first anniversary of his position as elder of the combined Berlin, Hanover and Vienna groups, decided to have a party in March of 1943. Concerts, plays, soccer matches, and now a party. And not just any party. Scrumptious cakes, cookies, sandwiches, wine and *Degvins*, a live band, and dancing. None of the inmates of the Latvian ghetto were invited but Zenta told me that she and the others had danced as if there was no tomorrow.

> *This was again living proof that we, Jews, were at some level in complete denial. Or maybe, it was our cry of resistance—probably, both. Don't you agree?*
>
> *That seems completely probable, Mr. Schwabe.*

---

[23] A work detail outside the ghetto

Anyway, despite my ardor, I constantly had to remind myself that my first love was only thirteen and that Zenta had to be treated accordingly. In fact, she was part of the young girls still of school age in the German ghetto; yet, Zenta would be continuing her studies for only another year, given after fourteen the ghetto children joined the work force. By summer of 1943, when there were hardly any schools left, the children's formal education ended even earlier, and upon reaching twelve, they were sent to work in the city or if not they usually tended the ghetto's vegetable gardens. Unfortunately, Svetlana and Rebecca, living in the Latvian ghetto, no longer enjoyed the luxury of attending school at all, since there were only twenty to thirty children of varying ages left, following both the pogroms. Thus, the remaining children were tutored instead on a very flexible basis. In the Latvian ghetto, now, the only moment, according to Svetlana and Rebecca, for which they really waited impatiently, was lunchtime, when they received their meager soup bowl from which they licked every last drop. They told me, too, that it was awesome listening to the sad clumping of all the children's wooden shoes as they left the kitchen with resignation until the next day. By contrast, all the youngsters in the Vienna group attended school beginning as early as four and were taught by "*Tante* Mary" Korwill at No. 5 Berliner Strasse; many of the young, including Zenta, had formerly attended her summer camp in Austria. *Tante* Mary used a monitorial system where the older students aided the younger ones. Since there was little paper, next to no books and even few pencils, Zenta told me that the children were forced to learn much by rote and memorization. My girlfriend confided also to me that one day when she was feeling particularly anxious and was sent to the blackboard, with her piece of chalk, she couldn't resist writing that singular question: "Will I die?" *Tante* Mary tried to reassure her. Actually, *Tante* Mary was reputed by both the parents and by Zenta and the other children for her kindness, devotion, and patience. However, by March, she suddenly fell out of the good graces of *Kommandant* Krause, who had learned that she had not turned over her gold wristwatch. He took her to the cemetery and shot her; he was also especially reputed for the murder of female ghetto members. Renowned also for his sadism, he could not resist bringing Mary's aged mother along to watch her daughter's gruesome execution.

In the meantime, Lange usually killed his victims, again out of spite, on the *Sabbath*. Afterwards, like Jekyll and Hyde, he brought some chocolate to the children playing in the sandbox. Similarly, at Auschwitz, Josef Mengele, was nicknamed affectionately by the children, "Uncle Pepi". He too indulged them with chocolates and other sweets. Afterwards, he invited the youngsters for a ride in his car, delivering them without any remorse to the gas chambers. *Doctor, I hate to admit it, but all of these incidents made me begin to lose faith in mankind.*

In any case, in the ghetto's gaslight world, when Zenta learned that Tante Mary was murdered, she never seemed entirely the same; she became depressed and pessimistic. Elizabeth Bergmann, a Czechoslovakian, was *Tante* Mary's replacement. Although she too was meritorious, Zenta was still heart broken because *Tante* Mary had become a second mother for her. Anyhow, private lessons were also given to those who could afford them, which was obviously not Zenta's case. Several times a week for a modest piece of bread, Dr. Weil, a former professor of literature at the University of Vienna also gave lectures on Goethe's *Faust* to some of the older ghetto members. In the midst of the Holocaust, the ghetto members maintained many of their former habits as well as their thirst for culture, which, on the other hand, I found most impressive.

The Berlin group, the Leipzig, and the Düsseldorf groups had relatively large schools. Other groups which had fewer children such as the Cologne and Kassel groups, eventually combined forces and created one school. Whatever the group, when the children returned home from school, they were consumed by other chores. The older ones having made a fire would prepare the evening meal for their elders, others acted as messengers, and again others helped to clean the houses and streets.

Meanwhile, my romance with Zenta continued passionately. Yet, we resisted having sex with each other. However, at night before going to sleep, I masturbated. When I woke up in the morning, almost inevitably I also found myself in a puddle of urine. And as for Zenta, almost every time I thought about her I had an erection. Why did we not simply have sex together? On the one hand, we realized we were too young and more importantly we did not want to take the risk of a pregnancy. During the first year, there were a few normal births; the babies were immediately killed by an injection; the mothers were told that the infants had been born stillborn. Only one child had survived and only temporarily, Ben Ghetto, Son of the Ghetto. But even he suffered the same fate as the others. Furthermore, during the summer of 1942, as abortions had increased, sex was even forbidden in the ghetto. *Only the Germans would be stupid enough to think they could enforce such a rule. You must agree with me, Doctor. Posters were placed on the doors of all the houses stating that sex was VERBOTEN. Can you imagine?* At this time, too, doctors were lecturing us teenagers, about diseases and contraception. Dr. Rolf Bischofswerder, a physician from Cologne warned Zenta and the other girls that should they become pregnant, they risked sterilization. Soon after, Krause ordered all women who were to undergo a second abortion to be sterilized. An abortion which was referred to as an "Appendicitis with Arms and Legs" was however taken seriously since Krause insisted that any man responsible for a pregnancy was given from ten to twenty-five lashes, administered either at the hospital or at the police station. If the woman refused to give the name of her partner, which occurred frequently, she had to suffer through her operation without anesthesia. In order to diminish these incidents, a clandestine hospital was created in the Kassel sector of the German ghetto.

Unfortunately, it was too small to accommodate all the pregnant women.

Marriage, like sex, was also forbidden in the ghetto, which was at least more understandable. However, this notwithstanding, ghetto weddings did occur. In fact, had we been older, there is no doubt we would have married, a plan which we postponed for later. Lurie, a Latvian Jew, in fact a friend of Mother's, was the ghetto's jewelry designer and engraver and even created wedding rings for the ghetto's couples who were planning to marry. They were always made of silver, sometimes with gold plating or a gold edge. On the inside he engraved the initials of the couple and the date of their marriage. Even at fifteen, an eternal romantic, without telling anyone, not even Abrasha, I bought one of Lurie's wedding rings which I gave to Zenta. Our initials were already engraved and I told her that we would later engrave the date when the war was over and we were finally old enough to marry.

Otherwise, the rings were not only used as wedding bands but had become one of the ghetto's fashion symbols. Lurie's shop was located in a clothing depot for the German air force, where many of the Germans also ordered rings. Albeit his prices were expensive, he always gave a discount whenever a band was solicited by an amorous ghetto couple, such as ourselves.

However, in certain cases, some logistic problems occurred with ghetto marriages. When the couple both lived in the same part of the ghetto, it was relatively simple; the woman changed her last name, usually combining it with that of her husband and the couple moved in with each other. Yet, when they did not reside in the same section, it became difficult for the ghetto bureaucracy to justify the change of address, particularly in a society where both marriage and sex were forbidden. The problem arose particularly between the Latvian men and the Reich women who like Tristan and Isolde were also separated, not by a sword but by barbed wire. In these frequent cases, the couples got together in the

German ghetto on Sundays when we, the Latvian men, could acquire the necessary pass to enter it.

Meanwhile, *Kommandant* Krause, a womanizer of the first order, was reputed for his affair with Olly Adler, a beautiful young Jewess who had arrived on the same transport from Vienna as Zenta. Krause was first thunderstruck by her one winter day when she was cleaning the snow. In Frederick Forsyth's novel, *The Odessa File*, he inaccurately attributed this romance to Eduard Roschmann, who succeeded Krause as ghetto *Kommandant*. While Olly trotted around the ghetto in her high heel shoes, Krause authorized her to run the ghetto's only beauty parlor on Prager Strasse; it was complete with all the amenities, whether hair dryers, wash basins or mirrors. Even though their relationship was considered *Rassenschande* (racial shame) and the usual punishment was death for the Jew and prison or death for the Aryan partner, they both seemed undeterred by the consequences. Krause also saw to it, as was often the case, that Olly's sister, Gerda Hacker, was assigned to a labor detail, something which was considered enviable in the sense that it allowed her to obtain food with a minimal amount of difficulty. However, in the long term, Olly's attractiveness was her downfall. After the liquidation of the ghetto, she was sent along with many of the others to Camp Kaiserwald where Hans Hannes, one of the Gentile professional criminals became totally bewitched by her. Emilie Kowa, the SS overseer of women who hoping to become Hannes' mistress, was consumed by jealousy and reported it. Consequently Olly, the *femme fatale*, was jailed in Riga's Central Prison and executed in the summer of 1944. Otherwise, their situation was not unique. *Oberwachtmeister* Neumann had a girlfriend from the Leipzig group with whom he had a frequent clandestine rendezvous in the garden in the back of No. 17 Berliner Strasse. Even Krause's chauffeur, Gymnich, could not resist the charms of one of the Jewesses from the Cologne group. Rumor had it that he even smuggled letters from her to her Gentile friends in the Reich.

While for some love seemed to conquer all, it must not be forgotten that all of us, Jews, were simultaneously in constant fear for our survival. Conditions in the ghetto remained atrocious, between the killings and punishments on the one hand and the starvation on the other. Each of us only received two hundred and twenty grams of bread each day, one portion of fish per week, an occasional portion of turnips, sour cabbage, or frozen potatoes and very sporadically a helping of horse meat. The few small children who were alive received only one liter of fat-free milk per week. The various illnesses also took their toll, be it typhoid fever, dysentery, typhus, tuberculosis or festering skin infections, often from lice. If the patients who were in the hospital did not recover within a three-week period, they were shot.

Furthermore, by early February 1942, the ghetto was to undergo another selection, followed by a similar one in the middle of March. This time it was almost predominantly the German ghetto Jews who were victimized, although until now they had been convinced that they were impervious. The first selection involved only the Berlin and Vienna groups. For the second selection, all the ghetto's ten groups were involved; each group's office was required to recommend people who were not part of the labor force, due to age, health or parents with small children. In both selections, the ghetto members were being sent supposedly to the town of Dünamünde, where they were supposed to work in comfortable inside jobs in the fish canneries; the town of Dünamünde, we were later told, had no longer been in existence for several decades.

Our longstanding Viennese friend, Emil Loebl was to be in charge of the second transport. We all felt so badly for both him and his daughter, Inge. She had suffered from frostbite as a result of the unheated car which had recently brought them to Riga from Vienna; consequently, upon arrival in Riga both her feet were amputated. Looking at this beautiful young girl unable to walk of course made me wonder how I would have felt had Zenta been on that same transport from Austria. Watching Inge made me really believe that life was an arbitrary fall of the dice.

In the meantime, Grandmother Chaija was no longer employed as a seamstress but was working instead in the *Gewerbebetrieb*, classifying the clothes. Grandmother explained to us that the Eastern Jews, such as ourselves, and particularly those from Poland, were renowned for traveling with their wealth upon them. They would arrive with entire trainloads of gold trinkets, diamonds, sapphires, rubies, silver, ingots, '*louis d'or*' coins, gold dollars and bank notes. They carried with them unimaginable amounts of wealth. What was not stolen by the SS was sent to Germany. Furthermore, I later learned that a portion of the profit in the form of gold bars engraved with the eagle of the Reich and the twin-lightening symbol of the SS was deposited towards the end of the war in the banks of Switzerland, Liechtenstein, Tangier and Bern, and formed the fortune on which the Odessa was later based. Much of the gold apparently still lies beneath Zürich's pavements, horded by the city's hungry bankers. Even hair was sorted out and sent back to the Reich to be turned into felt boots, while the gold fillings that had been yanked out of the victim's mouths were later melted down to be deposited as gold bars in Zürich. Lastly, at one point even the bones belonging to the Jews were sent back to the Reich for fertilizers and their body fats for soup until the Nazis decided this was uneconomical.

Anyhow, sorting through the piles of personal effects of the recently murdered, among the baby carriages, pocket books, shoes, and even the girdles still attached to stockings and turned inside out, Grandmother found in a school girl's blue blazer, Inge's I.D. card a week after her transport had left. We were then all faced with the reality that Gerhard Maywald's Dünamünde was one more Nazi deception. I later further read that in his trial in Hamburg during the winter of 1977, Maywald was quite proud of the lie that he had invented, believing that he was some sort of a saint, who, by having pacified his victims, spared them much pain. For me, this exemplified the Germans' *mauvaise foi*[24].

It was also at this time that without any warning, one evening as we were returning from work, Abrasha was arrested, with no reason given, as was often the case. Two months later in the late spring, he was suddenly released and returned to the apartment one day, completely out of the blue. Like Grandfather, earlier, he too seemed completely broken. He explained to me that he had been part of a labor detail consisting of thirty-eight Jewish men who were incarcerated along with the others at Riga's Central Prison. They were regularly taken to the Rumbula Forest to bury the victims of the two massacres. Their labor detail was alluded to as *Kommando Krause* 2. In addition, while they were in their cells, the Germans tried to brainwash them by having them listen to a record two hours a day, warning them never to discuss their work in the forest. Of the group, only sixteen including Abrasha returned to the ghetto.

Another important aspect of ghetto life was revolt. The Latvian ghetto's elite was focused on the need for armed resistance. A movement was created and led by Ovsey Okun, formerly a textile factory owner in Dvinsk, and attorney Jacob Jewelson, recently the administrator of the financial department of the Jewish community in the large ghetto. They were assisted by Yitzhak Bag, an older member of the Latvian police, as well as some younger men from the Small Ghetto and some others from the Latvian police. Unfortunately, Jewelson and a group of Jews from the ghetto later came in contact with a Luftwaffe Lieutenant who offered to help them escape to Sweden. After they had paid for their trip with gold and jewels, when they boarded the ship they were greeted by Krause and realized that they were the victims

---

[24] Self-delusion.

of a *Gestapo* provocation. They were subsequently killed, Krause having received his habitual sadistic pleasure. This notwithstanding, at the time, they built hideouts and stored weapons and supplies in the Latvian ghetto in preparation for a future insurrection. At several places at work, some of the Jews stole weapons which they smuggled into the ghetto with the assistance of the ghetto police. When the transport workers went to the city with horse-drawn carts to collect food rations for the ghetto, they also returned there, whenever possible, with dismantled rifles, machine guns and ammunition which they hid in crates and smuggled into the ghetto in spite of the fact that they were accompanied by SS. Weapons, medicines, food and even SS uniforms and insignia as well as other essentials were brought there to be kept in safe keeping for the future uprising. Several intricate bunkers were constructed and a tunnel was begun which led to a cemetery outside the ghetto. In the meantime, a bunker housing the weapons was located on Vilanu Street in the backyard of one of the houses. In a second bunker at the far end of the ghetto, food and medicines were also stashed.

The problems really began in the beginning of October when a few of my older friends, men I had known since childhood in Jurmala, desired to join a partisan group in Eastern Latvia instead of participating in the revolt which had been planned. These dissident Latvian Jews were betrayed, running into an ambush once they left the ghetto; all eleven were eventually killed. In fact, one was caught and under torture told the Germans the location of the secret arms depot. The Germans, overridden by suspicion, subsequently made a surprise check inside the Small Ghetto. They discovered an arsenal of weapons and even a canon. The Germans also found a list of men who were involved in the plot as well as a map, outlining all the places of attack. Even though only a few of the police were surprisingly involved in the plan, the Germans arrested all forty-one members of the Latvian Jewish police, considering that even those not actively involved in the future uprising, were at least aware of it. On the last day of October, all of the Latvian police force wearing their blue caps with the yellow star of David were marched to Tin Square. All were machine gunned except for one who temporarily managed to escape. He hid in the cellar at Kassel Court where potatoes were being sorted; the workers attempted to conceal him, throwing old sacks over him but the SS soon found and shot him. Furthermore, pieces of the blood-soaked earth where the Latvian policemen had been shot were later collected by some of their former girlfriends, who placed the soil into small sacks and wore them sentimentally around their necks. Rudolf Haar, the Jewish deputy of the German police, was suspected of collaborating with the Nazis since numerous members of the German police had searched the Latvian ghetto for the weapons. Despite Haar's innocence, the girlfriends of the murdered Latvians saw to it that after his arrival at Camp Kaiserwald, he underwent a grueling death through prolonged drowning. I realized, had I been slightly older, that Zenta would certainly have been wearing that little bag of soil around her neck. Once again I reflected upon life's arbitrariness, questioning how God could exist.

In any case, albeit the Latvians in general were markedly anti-Semitic, this prejudice inherited from the Russians, some of the local Gentiles still risked their lives to protect us and this is something no one should forget. We discovered, though only after the war, that the Lipke family in particular had been extremely efficient in hiding the Jews. They concealed them in a specifically dug hiding place before they transferred them to other places in Riga or to the environs of Dobele. Fifty-three lives had been saved by this family; two of them being former schoolteachers of Abrasha and myself. In Riga, altogether one hundred and fifty Jewish lives were spared in this way during the war. Yet, in contrast, others such as Ann-Alma Polis or Andrejs Grambins were caught hiding several Jews each. While Polis was tortured and killed, Grambins was sent to Dachau and executed. I felt such gratitude towards these people and such frustration that to some I was never able to express it.

Mr. Schwabe, do you feel remorse concerning their deaths?

Yes, some, but especially a profound sadness.

In the meantime, we Jews often entrusted our valuables to Gentile friends before entering the ghetto. Some large sums of money and some of our jewels were being held by long time friends and patients of Grandfather. Though when the war ended we had the good fortune of recuperating everything we had left with them, many of our friends had been robbed; a few were even denounced by the Gentiles in order to keep the Jews' property and money. Actually, we, Jews, could never really be sure who we could trust. Yet, on the whole, there were very few.

In any case, life in the ghetto continued until suddenly one morning Abrasha and I having reported to our labor detail on Prager Strasse were told that our contracts had been cancelled. We were to return home, pack, and report to Tin Square at eleven the following morning. We were then informed that we were being temporarily relocated to the Liepaja ghetto because an extra team of electricians had been required for one of the German's housing projects. Although I was pleased with the idea of eventually rejoining my aunt and uncle as well as my cousins, I was destroyed at the thought of being separated from my other family members, Zenta and Rebecca. I was also very frightened that we were not leaving for Liepaja but instead for Dünamünde, as had the others.

The next day, when we arrived at *Skirotava* Station among the hustle and bustle of the transports, two ominous black freight cars awaited us, each car holding about ninety people. It was there too that I learned from one of the Latvian drivers that ninety percent of all the prisoners arriving at *Skirotava* Station on the various transports were immediately taken to Bikernieku and Rumbula forests to be murdered. According to the driver I had spoken to, some days as many as twenty-five blue buses left the station, taking the inmates to the nearby woods. Abrasha and I were appalled, never imagining that the pogroms had grown to this portion. We both agreed that under the circumstances, we would be more than fortunate should we reach Liepaja alive. Filled with angst, as the Germans locked us in, I recollect the guard threateningly scream "Remember ten for one". Although most of the men spoke in Yiddish, the *lingua franca* of the ghetto, they still formed a crazy Babel of Latvian, Polish, Czech as well as a small number of Lithuanian, Russian, and German Jews. In the back of the car, a group of them nestled together to protect themselves from the cold, singing Yiddish songs above the hellish clatter of the car. Repeatedly and relentlessly many sung the same melody "Girlie, lift up your little dress, show what you've got". Meanwhile, above the singing and the yelling, another bunch of Russian Jews were also fervently joining in with some patriotic songs such as the most famous one, *Moskwa Moya, Lubymoya* [Moscow, My Beloved]. Fortunately, these various concerts were relatively short lived, given that our voyage was only four hours instead of those endless trips from the Reich suffered by the others.

When we arrived, we were marched through the dark streets of Liepaja. Although most of the houses in the Bahnhofstrasse had been destroyed, a mixture of wooden and red brick ones still remained. Upon arrival at the ghetto we were given a number, which had been the practice there since the spring of 1942. Simultaneously, we were divided into various labor groups and housed in separate buildings, the living conditions actually more bearable than in Riga. The rooms were larger, containing a few army cots, an oven, a table and chairs. We immediately rushed around hectically trying to locate our other family members. We instead found some of their friends who told us about the atrocious pogrom which had been held at Skede in December of the preceding year and we learned that all of our family had met their brutal deaths there. We were both devastated and disoriented by their demise. As we had done after Grandfather's death, we grew beards during the traditional thirty-day period of mourning. Otherwise, our mission lasted only two months, and even though I was with Abrasha, I terribly missed all the women close to me... even Rebecca who had become a foster sister. But to look at the bright side... this was the first time in over a year we had not been dying of starvation, for the simple reason that Liepaja's ghetto was not closed to the Gentiles, who came frequently inside in order to have their clothes made. At such times, they brought food into the ghetto for the workers who generously shared it with us and the others. As the Latvian Jews consisted of many adept craftsmen and artisans, they were fortunately solicited even by the SS for their dressmakers, tailors and cobblers, and this was instrumental to our survival for the two months we spent there before returning to the Riga ghetto.

In June of 1943, Himmler had ordered the total concealment of all traces of the pogroms. At this time, a special work detail was formed in Riga initially under Lange's supervision known as *Kommando Stützpunkt*. Afterwards, the *Kommando* was entrusted to the colorless and inept Edourd Roschmann, who succeeded Krause as ghetto *Kommandant* in January of 1943. Roschmann, previously a lawyer in Graz, Austria, was the anti-hero of Forsyth's *Odessa File*. Most of the atrocities attributed to Roschmann by the author were in fact committed by his predecessor, Krause, who was uncontestedly considered to be the ghetto's butcher; he only lacked the white apron. Furthermore, unlike Krause, Roschmann usually did not kill his victims but instead sent them to prison because it was rumored that he was unable to shoot straight. Occasionally, Roschmann visited the hospital, but mainly he wandered, seemingly without purpose, around the ghetto. Before long, his only claim to fame became his supervision of *Kommando Stützpunkt*, registered methodically under file number 105, for all countries where Germans and their helpers had massacred Jews.

The members of the detail had to exhume the bodies from their mass graves in the forests, build up cremation pyres, stack the corpses in piles and incinerate them. Parallel seven meter long pits were dug and a cover of thick boards would be placed over them. Then a layer of corpses would be put on the top and poured over with kerosene and flipped over back and forth as if they were hamburgers being prepared for a barbecue. No respect for our dead. None. It was shameful. We also learned from either the German drivers or the civilians that workers for this grisly job were taken to the forest once a week or every two weeks. Ten men were taken away, from either ghettos or camps, shackled together, and then bound from the waists to the ankles with two kilogram chains, making it impossible for them to escape. This work *Kolonne*, consisted mainly of men only. Sometimes, some of them were included as a form of punishment. In 1944, a group of men, as was often the case, had been duped that they were to join a work detail to stuff mattresses. Instead, they were taken to the forest for exhuming the bodies. Our beloved Lurie was among them and, like the others, never returned. Since the Rumbula pits were only about a hundred yards from a major railroad, neither the smoke nor the stench could be hidden from the travelers coming in and out of Riga... no less the Latvians, themselves. At this point everybody in Riga began to realize what had really happened. Many were horrified.

Meanwhile, in Riga plans had been made by the German authorities as early as April to dispatch large contingents of healthy and able men to work in the numerous peat bogs throughout the country. Starting in May 1943, various groups had been sent and to my total dismay, Abrasha was one of the men arbitrarily chosen. My brother and myself were faced once again with the same solitude created by our first separation of the preceding year. When in autumn we were reunited in Kaiserwald, Abrasha related to me the grueling details of his mission. On starvation rations and without any possibility of "organizing" any extra food, he and the others lived in very elementary huts like animals and were forced to undergo a twelve-hour day without food. When they wanted to relieve themselves at a nearby ditch, the guards would release their half wild Alsatian dogs, which often tore his co-workers to shreds. Thus, the men, both terrified and humiliated, did not usually budge an inch during the seemingly endless days. By evening, they were thus overwhelmed by the stench of urine and excreta, not to mention their starvation and exhaustion.

On the other hand, it was springtime, and with it, at least, for some of the ghetto inmates, came a relative sense of optimism. The maple trees and the white birch trees, sacred to the ancient Latvians were surrounded by long sweeps of lilac bushes in full bloom. Simultaneously, the foliage of the vegetable gardens announced an even more abundant produce than the previous year. Several of the groups had built public baths, which were very much in demand even though they contained only a primitive kind of shower and possibly one bathtub; only the Latvian ghetto had a real public bath and showers. Meanwhile, the food rations were improved; horsemeat being given more frequently.

At work in the electrical company, I also learned from some Latvian co-workers that many of the Latvians were expecting to gain their freedom from the Germans. Albeit thus far they had not succeeded, at least, in the winter of 1943 a decree for restitution of property was issued. Notwithstanding that large industrial and commercial companies had been kept under German control, some individuals did have property returned, though contingent upon signing an affidavit in which they agreed to work in the interest of the German nation. When some of the wealthy Latvians had their family castles restituted, they were at first convinced there was a light at the end of the tunnel. Yet, this illusion was somewhat short-lived when immediately after their sons between nineteen and twenty-four who had not volunteered were illegally drafted. Was this not reminiscent of the Russians?

Apart from the return of property, the Latvians were again filled with hope when, as of the summer of 1943, their national song festivals were once again permitted. In July a large concert, really a happening, of two thousand sung for an audience of four thousand in Riga. The program, very nationalistic in flavor, included numerous emotionally filled folksongs as well as a *cantata* by Andrejs Jurjāns entitled *Tēvijai* (For the Fatherland). A couple of weeks later, forty-five choirs and one thousand six hundred singers partook in a regional festival in Jelgava. Did the Latvians not fail to realize that Hitler and the Nazis were just giving them crumbs, manipulating them to obtain maximal support for the war effort? Not only were they despicable but they were naïve, or worse, stupid.

Furthermore, in the summer or perhaps as early as spring of 1943, Himmler decided to abolish the ghetto system that had been established in Eastern Europe and transfer us to nearby concentration camps. I was later told that this decision was taken by him upon the advice of Ernst Kaltenbrunner, Heydrich's successor, since he believed that the relationship between us and the Germans had become too close. This I found unbelievable after all the pogroms. For me, it was evidence of pure paranoia and delusion. In any case, Kaltenbrunner believed that too many Jews had too much power, being employed in one way or another in positions of importance and confidence by the Germans. He thought our lives were also too cushioned and therefore we were not being destroyed as we should have been by hard labor. Furthermore, the uprising in the Warsaw ghetto in April of 1943 was probably the straw that broke the camel's back. Anyway, by the end of 1943, with the exception of the Litzmannstadt ghetto in the Warthegau and the Kovno ghetto in Lithuania, both of which existed until the summer of 1944 as well as a few others scattered here and there, the ghetto system was for all intents and purposes terminated, to be replaced by concentration camps. Thus, the liquidation of our ghetto began in May 1943 and was not completed until November of the same year. Most of the other ghettos such as Vilno, Liepaja, Minsk, Cracow, to name a few, occurred much more quickly, having taken a maximum of six weeks. In any case, most of the inhabitants of the liquidated ghettoes in Dvinsk, Liepaja and Vilnius were moved to Kaiserwald by the end of 1943. By then, almost all the Jews, especially the old, the children and the sick were killed or, if they could work, sent to concentration camps.

At the end of August when I reported to my labor detail on Prager Strasse, I was once again told like many months before that my contract had been annulled and that I was to go home and return the next day with the essential belongings that I could carry with me. I soon realized that this time my relocation was somewhat permanent and unfortunately no longer to another ghetto but instead to Kaiserwald, the newly constructed concentration camp in Mezaparks, formerly a luxurious suburb on the outskirts of Riga. The camp had numerous branches in Veemilgraves, Spilve, Strazumizā, the "Lenta" factory, Sarkandaugava, Strasdinof and Dundaga where I spent time, not to mention a few of the others. Ironically, near the woods where the camp had been built, my family and friends had in the past gone skiing on winter weekends and the high school classes of my school also played soccer in the autumn and spring seasons. Again our lives were filled with these bitter contrasts which were completely unpredictable, unfathomable, and illogical.

In any case, the following day I reported to Tin Square awaiting my transfer to "another camp". Under the auspices of our cherished Fleischel and the Jewish police, I stood there, bundled up in winter clothing, including my winter coat and three or four sweaters and carrying a suitcase worth of personal effects packed into a huge sack. With a group of other men, we began the six mile walk to Camp Kaiserwald; looking as if we were part of a vaudeville, we marched fatalistically along. As we passed different locations where Jews worked, we begged for water and were often even given some. This was, however, strongly discouraged, because both Fleischel and the Jewish police were fearful that our requests would provoke the nervousness of the SS, who were consequently capable of shooting us. Anyway, there was much criticism of the Germans when the Latvians were finally faced with the reality of our fate and as a result the future transports were made by bus, presumably the same ones which had taken so many Jews to their death and would continue to do so. When I remember this interminable walk, I always think of Fleischel, of his goodness and of his leadership. A few weeks later he sadly died of cancer of the stomach and for once and maybe the only time, the Nazis apparently honored the death of a Jew. His funeral I was told was likened by some to a "state funeral"; his coffin was carried through the ghetto, followed by his bereaved wife, many ghetto members and even a large number of Nazis. Commanded by Krause, three volleys were shot at the old cemetery. Meanwhile, German Jews were hanging on Tin Square. The Nazis were at least always consistent in their contradictions.

THE CONCENTRATION CAMPS AND THE EUTHANASIA CENTERS

It is important to remember that the first concentration camps existed only in Germany and were different from the later ones, both those within the country and those outside of it, such as Kaiserwald. While the earlier ones were created for the most part for the political opponents of the National Socialists by the SA, the later ones were constructed by the ruthless SS predominantly for us, Jews, but also for the other races which the Nazis considered inferior, such as the gypsies, who though much less numerous were treated almost as badly. Criminals were also among the Nazi targets as well as the shiftless asocials which included vagrants, touts, pickpockets, tinhorn gamblers, pimps, deadbeat fathers, and prostitutes, to name only a few. Political adversaries were still, of course, part of those deemed worthy of incarceration.

I later also learned that, regarding the earlier camps, Goering clearly stated that these were established to isolate, defame, humiliate, crush, and annihilate all enemies of the National Socialists; the Communists being viewed as particular offenders. While the major goal of the earlier camps was punishment or isolation, many of the later ones were focused primarily on the extermination of Jews. The later camps were on the whole much more brutal, which apart from the evolving political situation was due to the SS. Important, too, although the SS initially consisted of men with an outstanding social pedigree, it quickly was comprised of others from all walks of life and often the dregs. Furthermore, like their founder Heinrich Himmler, their intellectual development was far below average.

Consequently, their sense of inferiority turned quickly to arrogance, one of the classic veneers for hatred and we Jews became their scapegoats.

> *Mr. Schwabe, it is not only during W.W.II, but also throughout history that the Jews have been scapegoats. Why, according to you?*
>
> *It is obvious that our success has provoked much jealousy. Otherwise, it is not a question with a simple answer. Maybe, due to our achievements, many considered us to be arrogant. I really do not know.*

Otherwise, the original camps were organized as of 1933, in the vicinity of Berlin. This notwithstanding, Dachau, built in 1934, was one of the most notorious, situated an hour outside of Munich. In fact, after the war I was told that the inmates sent to any of the camps were generally alluded to as being sent "to Dachau", even the later ones, outside of Germany such as our own. In any case, Kaiserwald, I was later informed, albeit the largest camp in the Baltic, was very modest next to a camp such as Buchenwald which was really equipped with all the amenities including a movie theater. For example, there was also a falconry court built as a tribute to Hermann Goering and a riding hall for the wife of the camp's *Kommandant*, Karl Otto Koch. The falconry court, which was no modest undertaking, took two years to construct. The price for only the materials was close to one hundred and thirty five thousand marks.

> *Can you imagine? You would think that the Nazis were building luxury hotels and not concentration camps.*

Anyway, as usual it all seemed very surrealistic. In addition, the area contained numerous buildings, comprising the falcon house proper, which was built in ancient Teutonic style consisting of massive but skillfully carved oak, a hunting hall with hand-carved oak furniture, an enormous fireplace overladen with hunting trophies, a circular garden house, and the falconers' abode, itself, where later, when the sport of falconry could no longer be practiced, the former French premier, Léon Blum and other prominent political figures were lodged. There was also a game preserve and a cage filled to the brim with various and sundry creatures such as wildcats, fallow deer, roe bucks, a wild boar, a mouflon, foxes, pheasants, monkeys, bears, and in the early years even a rhinoceros. After the war I was also apprised, when one of the animals died, that a "voluntary" collection was taken up among the poor Jews in order to subsidize a replacement. This was especially ironic as one of the sadistic pleasures of the SS was often to have the Jews torn limb from limb or eaten alive by the animals.

Why all this hatred?

Don't forget, Doctor, apart from everything we have already discussed together, many of those who worked in the camps were criminals projecting their frustration and hatred on to us, Jews.

At the end of the day, one could really wonder if the Nazis did not prefer animals to people. Can you believe while they were killing us off like flies, they were also doing everything under the sun to protect their four-legged companions? Hitler, for example, during his first three months in power, signed three separate laws on the protection and treatment of animals, with penalties for cruel treatment, mishandling, and misfeeding. In 1936 he even passed a regulation to reduce the suffering of lobsters and crabs, as well as other crustaceans, forbidding to have them killed other than by throwing them in rapidly boiling water before being served in restaurants, this being considered the least cruel method of killing them. Meanwhile, Goering drew up Reich hunting and forestry laws. He even promulgated an antivivisection law; offenders were to be sent to a concentration camp.

He further protected animals by preventing their use in medical research which he instead reserved for Jews.

In fact, both in Riga and in Kaiserwald, we, Jews were the human guinea pigs. As of 1942, many Jews were forced to participate in very dangerous experiments involving spotted typhoid fever, known to be transmitted by body lice. Many of these tests were executed under Dr. Abhagen of the Institute in Riga. In order to perfect his experiments, he even asked authorization from the German government to reduce the working hours of the Jews under experimentation; the human guinea pigs in question at least had the good fortune to have their working day reduced in half, in order that they might recuperate as quickly as possible so as to serve as blood donors over and over. Later, similar experiments were also held at Kaiserwald which were again focused on typhoid fever. Apart from a few of our friends, among those tested were several pairs of twins later killed with Abrasha at the time of the last selection in the summer of 1944. Even children were not spared, as revealed by postwar examination of their exhumed bodies in which various poisons were systematically found. I later learned that at Auschwitz, Dr. Mengele, the monster in charge of selections, was fascinated by twins. Was he not reputed for also testing them relentlessly in order to find out how to propagate the *Herrenrasse*?

Apart from this, many concentration camps had, as of the summer of 1943, brothels. A "Reich Directive" stated that brothels designated as "special buildings" were to be constructed. Eighteen to twenty-four girls from Ravensbrück were shipped to the various camps where these brothels were established. The women, many of whom were quite familiar with this profession, were all volunteers. Rumor had it that they were promised to be released after six months in exchange for their services. I further learned that when a prisoner did not have pull, his visit was limited to twenty minutes. One would have thought that the brothels were created for the purpose of entertaining the SS and the *kapos*. But not all. They were considered to be instead a means of distracting the inmates from political activity. The Nazis as usual had a logic all of their own.

The final solution to the "problem" of the Jews and their children was not limited to their ghettoization, nor by their removal to the concentration camps. Earlier, and known throughout the Reich, was the infamous "euthanasia project", specifically the petition for the "mercy killing" initially of an infant named Knauer, born blind with one leg and one part of one arm which was also missing; in addition the child was mentally impaired. Consequently, as of the summer of 1939, a law was passed stating that a child either mentally retarded or seriously deformed was to be killed. He was obviously not a candidate for Hitler's *Herrenrasse*. On the contrary.

By 1940 a network of some thirty killing areas within existing institutions were set up in Germany, Poland, and Austria. Those parents who showed reluctance received letters stating the irrevocability of the situation. This notwithstanding that most families refused withdrawal of their guardianship. Nevertheless after a few weeks, the children were usually killed by means of luminal tablets dissolved in a liquid such as tea. If the child was not killed fast enough, a fatal morphine called scopolamine was given to him by injection. As you can imagine, very quickly the Jewish children were brought into the net. Although the church and the families rebelled, and to a lesser extent even the medical profession, many children and soon in particular the Jewish children were as was said in the vernacular "put to sleep", like animals. Although many are aware of the concentration camps, euthanasia is generally less known. *Even you, Doctor, I imagine may never even have heard about it.*

Initially, children, but soon also the adults who were mentally ill and or retarded, and in particular the Jews of all ages were driven off in postal vans with the blinds pulled down. Many had to be put in strait jackets or handcuffed to get them into the buses. The destination of the vehicles was even kept secret from the medical staff who loaded them. In the meantime, letters were sent to their families, notifying them of the transfer, with the pretext that the change being effectuated was war-related. The six main killing centers were in Hartheim, Sonnenstein, Grafeneck, Bernburg, Brandenburg, and Hadamar. They were in isolated areas and had high walls. They were former mental hospitals or nursing homes. At least one had been a prison, and some were initially old castles. Once the patient had arrived in the killing center, a second letter was sent to his or her family, announcing the arrival and informing them that the shortage of personnel due to the war made their visit impossible. This letter was sent by the killing doctor or the head of the euthanasia center, and always signed with a false name. Lastly, the third letter was sent, again under a false name, by the Condolence-Letter Department, days or weeks later. Equally outrageous was the fact that families were often mixed up, and a family received two urns when only one family member was killed and vice versa. Other confusion involved gender; in the ashes of a male victim, hairpins were found, for instance. The cause of death was equally falsified. The only way that families could vent their wrath was by placing statements in the death columns to the effect: "His sudden death will always remain a mystery to us." Otherwise, systematic T4 treatment of German Jews began in April 1940, with a proclamation from the Reich stating that all Jews were to be inventoried within a three week period. Furthermore, either Jews, the mentally ill or the retarded, in total close to nine thousand, were killed in the gas chambers of the cellars of the Bernburg Psychiatric Hospital between September 1940 and August 1941. As with the camps, although we were not the initial targets, ultimately we were once again the Germans' inevitable scapegoat. When I learned this, I could only question if Father had been aware of what was happening in his country. I wondered too what would have been his reaction.

KAISERWALD

Towards evening we finally reached the camp. It had been constructed that same year by five hundred Gentile prisoners who had been brought from Sachsenhausen. However, by summer when the first inmates began to arrive, only sixty percent of the original inmates were alive. The cruel *Obersturmbannführer* Albert Sauer, previously the *Kommandant* of K.Z. Mauthausen in Austria, had been appointed to the leadership of Kaiserwald, seconded by the first camp "Elder", Reinhold Rosemeier, a former beer hall owner sent to life imprisonment for double murder. As you can see, we were keeping good company. Otherwise, the camp was run by the German SS and mainly career criminals alluded to as *kapos*. Meanwhile, the *kapos* of the women's group were SS known as *Blitzmädel* ("lighting girls"), convicted prostitutes and even some Jewish women, who were responsible for the women's barracks.

Anyway, after passing a tomato field, we soon reached a high wooden gate which opened onto the entrance of the grounds. Kaiserwald, itself, was a complex of a number of barracks organized into three sections. The first was at the main gate, the administrative section which housed the SS staff and the guards, generally Latvian, Ukrainian, or Lithuanian. Behind the administrative building were the women's and men's sections. There were three barracks for each sex. The men's and women's sections were divided by double rows of barbed wire. Upon arrival, we were ordered to proceed. We were rushed into a large barrack situated in the last section which was the "reception hall" for us, newcomers. There was a receiving committee of SS officers, a few Jews, but mostly Gentile, criminal and political prisoners. On the desk was a bouquet of red roses. Were they not Hitler's favorite flowers? One of the *kapos* then showed me the warrant for my arrest which read as follows: "duration of custody indefinite". Often, prisoners entering the camps were told as a matter of form that they were being incarcerated for a period of three to six months, even though the delay was obviously undetermined; regardless, it was known to be reassuring for the inmates to be given some time frame. In my case, I had absolutely no idea and was thus more destabilized than ever. I also thought of Father. Where was he? Why didn't he come to our aid? I also signed several forms stating that I owned nothing but what I was wearing. Afterwards, we lined up, one after another and were sent to the tables where we were asked to turn in any gold or other valuables that we might have in our possession; all pocket and wristwatches had to be thrown in a plastic container. When we were in the ghetto, Grandfather had given me his initialed gold pocket watch which he had received from his father. Having to forsake it broke my heart. It was my last family relic. I felt as if I was cutting off the umbilical cord with my past and with my family. I felt more destitute than ever. Everything was taken from us except for razors and eyeglasses, if we wore them.

Then we were lined up in rows of five in front of the barracks and were led to an enclosure where we had to undress and leave our clothes. As we were hurried into the shower room, we only had a razor, shaving soap in a wooden container and a shaving brush. Once inside the SS examined us for lice which so far none of us had... if instead they had waited a few weeks, they would have been really busy. We soon spent nearly every night at the foot of our bunk taking off the lice from our clothing. Anyway, the SS ordered us to strip and perversely examined the hair on each of us for lice. While they ordered all the men to be shaved, the women's hair was also cropped very short. Body hair was further removed and a horrible smelling solution was spread over our arms and pubic area. This procedure in concentration camp vernacular was alluded to as "delousing". Afterwards, we went into the showers, probably a sad prelude to the future, where the water was either freezing cold or scalding hot. With neither soap to wash nor a towel to dry ourselves, we were still hurried out of the showers, the *kapos* shrieking the habitual, *Heraus! Heraus*! Then, we were immediately thrown by another group of Gentile *kapos* all sorts of various and sundry clothing from the last transport. All of the garments allotted to us... underwear, socks, shirts, pants, jackets, whatever were almost inevitably ill fitting. The later newcomers were provided with striped prison clothes like those of the criminals, alluded to as zebras. In any case, we looked like badly dressed clowns or people poorly attired for a costume ball. We were also issued round visorless caps which we later had to doff in order to show our respect to the SS. Afterwards, we were assigned a number which had replaced our former names, more importantly, our former identity. The numbers started at five hundred. Why? Probably because there were five hundred inmates responsible for the creation of the camp. But this remains only an educated guess.

By the time I arrived, already eight thousand Jews had been incarcerated; I was given the number 8511. Our numbers were imprinted on small rectangles of white cloth on the left breast, where previously the Star of David had been worn. Next to it was an identifying triangle; Jews a yellow triangle, criminals green, political prisoners red, homosexuals pink, and asocials black. In order to minimize the chances for our escape, our jackets were painted with a white cross in front and back and our pants had a white stripe down the side.

After we were dressed, we returned outside again where, as upon our arrival, the "professional criminals", the *kapos* were stationed all over the camp and were still angrily screaming all sorts of obscenities at us while beating and kicking us whenever they could. Most were yelling at us that we were assholes or shits. I later realized that the curses thrown at us were almost inevitably related to the anal sphere as if they were trying to reduce us to some infantile stage before toilet training. Unlike the ghetto, the prisoners were no longer referred to by their former titles of office but were addressed with the degrading "*du*". We, too, were forced to use this form in speaking to one another, also an indication that they were attempting to debase us to the level of children; instead, it was now us, Jews, who were to call them *Herr* and *Doktor*. *Can you imagine?* In fact, the professional criminals of all the groups were considered to be the best adapted to camp life because they now often found themselves in a seemingly superior status to the one they had held outside of prison life; in many cases, they had also become the wardens of the judges and lawyers, of the elite who had incriminated them. This, of course, empowered them.

In our barracks, alluded to as blocks, where the rats jumped over our heads all night long, Mikush, the sadistic block elder of Block Number Three, gained much pleasure watching us do the diverse exercises imposed upon us. He ordered us to stand up, lie down, jump like a frog or squat dozens of times in a row in order to wear us out and especially to disgrace us. Furthermore, many of the men with whom I cohabited also perished during the "night alarms". There, we the prisoners were forced to stand in front of the barracks and after having given a signal, the *kapos* would begin their appalling sessions of brutality. They hit us with whips, clubs, chains, or rubber truncheons, while in the middle of the night we ran inside and outside of the barracks frenetically trying to avoid the *kapos* and other prison guards, who concealed themselves behind the doors or under the windows. Mikush was a short, broad-shouldered Polish political prisoner. Although he had been an officer in the Polish army, he was in fact nothing more than an hysterical criminal who never stopped screaming. He was also especially reputed for sending us out, usually half naked at midnight, to the bathhouse, two blocks away in the grueling cold. Leaving from or returning to the barracks, he swung at us with his rubber truncheon until some of us were practically mashed to smithereens. Until this day, I can still hear him shouting out, *Heraus! Heraus!*, as his truncheon moved from left to right, striking me and the others as we attempted to get through the narrow doorway. Mikush also reveled in making us undergo foot inspection. We had to stick our feet out in the bunks and he verified if they were clean; once again, like animals, we often found ourselves washing them with our saliva. Mikush obviously was in some way obsessed with cleanliness. I still ask myself if, in some unconscious manner, he was not actually trying to purify himself, to cleanse himself of his self-hatred which he had imputed to us. *But, once again, you're the shrink, not me.* In any case, as you can imagine, all of us, Jews, were now considered by him and the other Germans as sadistic, uninhibited, and unintelligent. We were also seen as an inferior race, addicted to sexual perversions, caring only for material goods and having absolutely no respect for ideals or for moral and intellectual values. That was the reputation given us by the Nazis. Yet, little did he and the others realize that their opinion of us was completely reciprocal. Debased as we were, unannounced to them, we too still judged them, and a few of us among the more educated and evolved even realized that their beliefs about us could only be due to a combination of brainwashing and projection.

In our block we slept three abreast in three tiered bunks, squeezed together on one narrow pallet with its small mattress, made of straw, usually two facing one way, the third facing the opposite direction. Our boots served as pillows; this was also a convenient way not to have them stolen. I slept on the lower bunk so I spent many sleepless nights, given that the straw from the upper ones fell on me all night long and prevented me from sleeping. Between this and the stench of the men's feet, even at night I had no respite. In other barracks, men slept in bags which were old and torn, filled with rotten straw on the bare soil; some not even having a blanket. I think in a way, this might have been better.

Each morning we were awoken at four and at five chased out of our block by Mikush in order to attend morning roll call. Standing for hours, we were counted and recounted as we were commanded to put "caps on" or "caps off". If any of our moves were not performed to the liking of the *kapos* or the SS, we were usually punished by being required to squat and remain in that same painful position for long periods of time. Afterwards, we were taken to Riga to work for the day, and upon our return there were spot checks at the gate by storm-troopers clad in their brown uniforms, often dead drunk. Anyone who was caught with the merest trifle was severely beaten, placed in confinement, or sometimes even shot. Before sleeping, we attended again the interminable roll call.

We also suffered terribly from lice and from hunger. At work, we always tried to "organize" a meager piece of bread, a potato, or any tidbit which, like a stray dog, we could find. One must remember that we were only given a third of a piece of bread with a pat of margarine or marmalade, a daily ration of soup, which contained an occasional floating piece of potato or cabbage.

After betrayal of a fellow prisoner to the SS or the *kapos*, the stealing of food among ourselves was considered by all of us the worst offense that could be committed. It was ruthlessly punished. The inmates gave their fellow Jews several beatings and socially ostracized the offenders. Additionally, food was considered by us as a symbol of security and was one of our main topics of conversation; we often conversed about our future meals after liberation. *As you know, Doctor, I'm still obsessed.*

Shortly after my arrival, I went daily to the doubled barbed wire fence between the men's and the women's section, but I could not find any of the women of my family, nor Rebecca, nor Zenta. I was overwhelmed by fear that they had been part of a selection and were on some "transport to heaven". Finally, a couple of weeks later, I saw a group of women who had just arrived in the camp carrying on their backs the habitual knapsacks with their bare necessities; regulations had even been passed whereby they were only allowed one change of underwear and two pairs of stockings. Many also had shawls wrapped around their heads, making it more difficult to individualize them. Mother, however, came to the fence that night informing me that everyone had arrived with the exception of Grandmother who had been hospitalized for dysentery.

Svetlana, Mother, Rebecca and Zenta were fortunately in the same barrack, but were the constant victims of Elsa, a German prostitute from Ravensbrück, who without pity strutted around in her black boots, hollering while whipping anyone in sight. The only compensation was that they were all sent to work in the *Vorburg*, formerly a chic neighborhood of Riga which was inhabited now solely by Germans. There, the Nazis established an enormous warehouse in which they brought all sorts of items from jewelry to furniture, anything that they had robbed from us, whether living or dead. Not surprisingly, under the strictest supervision of the SS, the Jewish prisoners retrieved any of the jewels or money that had been sewn into the clothing; if they, themselves, stole any of the valuables, they were faced with the death penalty. Rebecca and Zenta were part of the SS "Alfred Rosenberg" *Kommando*, where Jewish girls classified the paintings, carpets, carvings, tapestries, in fact, any similar art objects. Simultaneously, the SS would laughingly tell them that everything that they were cataloguing would be the foundation of the new fortunes of the SS, such as their own. Jeckeln, himself, avariciously spent endless hours sorting out the valuables with which he later enriched his family in Germany.

Apparently, there were also workshops for uniforms, ball gowns, corsets, and underwear, a furrier's atelier and gloves. I was told that all of the clothes produced in these workshops looked as if they had been designated for luxury stores in the major cities. But no way—they were all made for the exclusive use of the most important SS officers, their wives and their girlfriends. Furthermore, some of the warm clothing, in particular, which had been sent from Germany and donated for the soldiers on the eastern front also found itself there. However, most of these items were never seen by the soldiers since the SS couldn't resist keeping the fur-lined coats and boots in which they strutted around Riga like proud peacocks.

I was later informed by one of the last arrivals from the ghetto to Kaiserwald that Grandmother had probably been sent to Auschwitz. The ghetto was liquidated on November 2, 1943. I later learned that there was a selection in the Small Ghetto by Lange and Krause and another in the Large Ghetto by Krause and Gymnich. During the process, Lange shouted sadistically at those who were to be shot: "Faster, faster to Palestine! Throw a glance at your arms depot!" Among those killed was the violinist Prof. A. Metz. Apart from those who were sent to Kaiserwald, the others were dragged from their hospital beds, like Grandmother, or their ghetto apartments and taken to *Skirotava*. There, over two thousand men, women, and children as well as the infirm were loaded into cattle cars at the marshaling yard and mainly transported to Auschwitz. Yet, some cars apparently never left Riga station and the Nazi victims were left mercilessly to freeze to death. Soon after, the ghetto hospital itself became a crematorium. Today, I still have nightmares where my beloved grandmother is being sent to her death by Mengele, wearing his habitual white leather gloves[25] as he blows his whistle and points his thumb to the right, sending my aged grandmother to her death.

Grandmother's demise sensitized me to the plight of the weak, of the children in particular. The children born at Kaiserwald, as in the other camps, were routinely killed by nurses. They were poisoned, strangled, dropped into cisterns, smothered with pillows. The nurses also pinched the baby's nostrils when it opened its mouth to breathe, in order to give it a dose of a lethal product. But

---

25 Leather gloves were for the Nazis a symbol of dignity.

what was even worse were the older children who found themselves parentless. By late 1943, Kaiserwald was populated by sixty children from two to twelve who had been transported from all over Europe, whether Prague, Vienna, Brno, Kovno, Pskow or Germany. Excuse my tears, but there are some I remember so vividly as if it was yesterday. Among them, there was little Abka with his deeply set, suffering eyes. His father was a cobbler who was killed in the Dvinsk ghetto. Abka was ill with pneumonia and in the hospital. Despite this, he snuck out and escaped through a hole in the barbed wire. Although he had been temporarily hidden, he had been inadvertently reported by a Nazi child and sent to Kaiserwald. There he became a prisoner and wore the striped uniform like all the others. Slated for death in one of the *Aktions*, we managed to save him by sewing him for a short period of time into a mattress.

Nine-year-old Jacob was another example of the orphans who had reached the camp. His father, mother, and older brother had been killed in the Ponar Forest and he was brought from the Vilna Ghetto. At one of the selections, a Latvian SS beat on his head because he tried to sneak away from the column of those chosen to die. Afterwards, the guard pushed Jacob in the direction of the other children. When for a moment the guard was looking in another direction, the boy managed to sneak into the row of adults leaving the camp for a work detail. A few weeks later, however, when the children from other camps were brought to Kaiserwald and sent to the forest in a truck, despite the fact that Jacob jumped over its side, this time he could not escape his fate... But there were so many other children with similar tales. Whenever I think about them, apart from their survival instinct, they all seemed to share one common quality—courage.

This was also manifested by their behavior with regards to the *kapos*. Each of the criminals had his own child servant who performed certain tasks such as polishing his boots, running errands, making his bed or cleaning his room. Sometimes, too, the children were sent to deliver love letters or packages to the female division, since it was easier for them to gain entrance to the women's barracks, as they could feign to be visiting a family member. Usually illegal, these expeditions often resulted in the children being beaten by the German or Latvian guards who attempted to make them confess the identity of their patrons. None of us had ever heard of even one betraying his master. Nonetheless, the *kapos* rarely showed any gratitude and treated the children perversely, teasing them, for instance, with a loaf of bread, and the minute they grabbed for it, removing it. In any case, their bravery and loyalty remained unwavering in the midst of this overwhelming adversity. Their behavior admittedly reinstilled my faith in mankind. It was probably because of them that I have never given up.

> *I imagine, Mr. Schwabe. that this must have been one of your principal motivations for having children... Do you agree?*
>
> *Certainly, and you will never believe how proud I am of them.*

However, even at Kaiserwald, like the ghetto, there was still some recreation. On Sunday afternoons, sometimes we would play ball in the little meadow. Rather than soccer, basketball had now become the favorite sport. Why the change? No one really knew. Maybe the murder of the Jewish Latvian police had left a bad taste in too many mouths. In any case, teams from the various blocks enthusiastically fought each other, while other inmates relaxed during the warmer months on the grass or elsewhere inside during the winter season. On Sunday nights we usually had a concert in one of the large shops in the factory where there was a dilapidated piano badly out of tune, several violins, and even a slightly battered accordion. The orchestra consisted of former professional musicians who played with fervor

Beethoven, Haydn, Mozart, Rimsky-Korsakov and any other modern composer you could think of. When summer began and liberation seemed around the corner, Russian music was played progressively more often. "*Moskva Moya, Lubimaya*" and other Russian songs soon took precedent. Otherwise, we sometimes acquired two-hour passes allowing us to visit the women's barracks. These were the privileged moments when I visited my family and Zenta and Rebecca.

Svetlana and Mother, actually even Rebecca and Zenta, had been marked by Grandmother's death. When we were together on the occasional Sunday I spoke nostalgically with my mother and sister about Jurmala and our family outings with Grandmother and Grandfather, remembering the barbecues on the beach as well as the other family gatherings. It was then, too, I spent the little time allotted to me with Zenta. Although her long hair had been cropped and she was completely emaciated, my lust for her still remained very much alive. Maybe I was still a healthy adolescent? Even though I was later told that in general it was usually only the SS, the *kapos*, and the cooks, those who were among the best fed, who had any remaining sex drive, I was among the inmates who was one of the exceptions who seemingly broke the rule. When we met, we often spent a few intimate moments in the neighboring woods. Zenta explained to me that she was worried because she no longer had her periods. Had I retrieved myself in time? I confided to her that I frequently tried to masturbate but to no avail. Apparently, I had become impotent. Later, I learned that her failed periods and my impotence was only normal, given the psychological stress we were undergoing. Apparently in the Soviet camps, people had fewer sexual problems and more activity because they lived in conditions that were relatively better. As usual, we spoke much about our former lives and our future hopes. Little about the present; the camp conditions, as you might have gathered, being much worse than even in the ghetto.

Otherwise, among many of the Nazi anomalies, the books which had become unobtainable throughout the Reich were available in the camps and could be read illegally at Kaiserwald. They were among the books recovered from the German wastepaper collections; the Nazis having appropriated many libraries of "enemies of the state" and turned them over to these collections, when they were not burned. Given Zenta and I were avid readers, whenever we could get our hands on one of the classics we relished upon it, always spending some of the little time we had together speaking about Plato, Heine, Klabund, or Möhring, among many.

Anyhow, when we couldn't get our two-hour pass to the women's section or could not play basketball or listen to a concert, Sundays became for us the most dreaded day of the week because in order both to humiliate and exhaust us, under Mikush's direction, we spent the day loading and unloading the sand or stones unto nearby trucks which we then reloaded a few meters away and lugged back to the starting point. At other times some of us were forced to work at night at the *Anoden Kommando*, one of the numerous organizations that earned money from slave labour. There, throughout the wee hours of the morning, we dismantled batteries that the Germans planned to readapt and recycle. This was also no piece of cake because by morning, myself and the others were hardly recognizable, looking like chimney sweepers all covered with soot.

Meanwhile, when Abrasha returned in September 1943 from the peat bogs, not surprisingly more pessimistic than ever, he was assigned to another block, where the block elder, Xavier Abel, was notorious for being as brutal as Mikush. Abrasha and I really had bad luck. Xavier Abel called himself Mr. X, for what reason no one really knew. However, given the level of his criminality, it was probably sensible for him to maintain a low profile without any identity, but we all agreed this was certainly not his motivation. Previously, however, he proudly informed Abrasha and the others in his barrack that he had been a member of the S and B gang in Berlin, where he had been sentenced to life imprisonment for a double murder. Abrasha told me that, like the others, he was terrified of him, given that his ruthlessness had no limits. In fact, he was specialized in throwing people into the Daugava River and not permitting anyone to rescue them. One day, according to my brother, Mr. X was alleged to have thrown one of the Jews into the Daugava, simply because he didn't like the way he looked. When the man tried to swim and attempted to hold on to a nearby boat, Mr. X kicked away his hands and the Jew nearly drowned. Eventually, Abel allowed the man's friends to pull him out, but this notwithstanding, his victim died a few days later. Similarly, another Jew was beaten to death by him in the boathouse merely because he felt that the inmate had not washed himself properly. One of the most shocking performances occurred when Mr. X threw a prisoner who had dysentery and had given his food to another prisoner into a kettle of boiling water that was used for the inmates' coffee. The ailing prisoner was boiled to death and coffee was served as usual. After recounting this last tale of woe, Abrasha confided to me that, with everything he had recently seen and lived through, he thought that he was losing his mind and he had little to no desire left to live. A week later, he made a failed suicide attempt, having taken poison, but fortunately not enough. Consequently, as was the rule for those who tried to kill themselves, he was given twenty-five lashes and kept for a period in solitary confinement.

At the end of September when two transports reached Kaiserwald, one from the Riga ghetto and one from the Vilno ghetto, I learned from one of my school friends, Lieba, that upon his arrival at Kaiserwald, the *kapos* arranged "a sour night". The Jewish male prisoners were forced to run in circles inside their barracks, while the criminal prisoners stood on wooden tables and with clubs and whipped and beat them mercilessly. When I found Lieba a few days later, he looked totally battered and was also blinded in one eye. Having drunk schnapps and vodka, the Germans continued to torture them until the morning roll call at which time they stood at the doors and once again struck the Jews as they were leaving the barracks in order to be counted. The women, including Zenta, as she later reported, were terrified by the cries and screams which continued relentlessly throughout the night. The wailing was so loud that it could be heard across the barbed wire in the women's barracks. All of them, according to my girlfriend, felt impotent, knowing that they were unable to do anything at all to assist their menfolk. Zenta admitted to me that she could only pray that I was not among them.

Otherwise "sour night" was proof that the German criminals could only feel empowered by debasing us. The more we were dehumanized, by definition, the wider the gap between them and ourselves. The more subhuman we became, the easier for them to treat us with absolute indignation, given the cleavage between us and themselves had grown so great, that conveniently we could then be viewed by them as mere "items" or "pieces". Our dead were often even alluded to irrespectively as "cargo". After all, in their eyes, had we not become mere two-legged objects? It was consequently even simpler for the *kapos* as well as the SS to render us the scapegoats for their pent-up anger, hatred and frustration.

Anyhow, these transports were followed by an especially affluent one including particularly wealthy Jews, among them friends of Aunt Clara and Uncle Clarence who had been supportive and hospitable to Abrasha and myself during our sojourn in the Liepaja ghetto. They were laden with jewels, gold, silver... it was the cavern of Ali Baba *par excellence*. As you can imagine this was a real feast, better yet an orgasm, for the SS. Upon arrival, the women, always known for being more clever at concealing their valuables than the men, hid their jewels, money and any other precious items in the straw-filled mattresses, not realizing that the initial quarters assigned to them were only temporary. They never suspected that only two hours later, they were to be relocated elsewhere. Meanwhile, the SS searched their barracks and returned avariciously with a huge basket filled with gold which they proudly displayed. Notwithstanding their immediate and unexpected, impoverishment, the Liepaja Jews were otherwise viewed as a great asset, given that they acted as a welcomed bridge between the Riga Jews and the Reich Jews, as they spoke German.

It was soon Christmas Eve. Another selection, and sixty Jews who were ill were sent to the right and to their death. Their demise was probably the Christmas gift that the Nazis gave to themselves. A ritual offering, why not? The next day, the Nazis, filled with Christmas spirit, gave us half a day off and a feast of sausages and potato salad. All that was missing was Santa Claus himself! Sauer and the other SS and *kapos* were still very drunk and insisted on a concert in assembly square, which was lit up by glittering swastika ornaments on the surrounding pine trees. With our makeshift instruments we formed a band and disheartedly played Christmas music to appease the Germans.

Otherwise, three months earlier, fifty German female prisoners had been brought from Ravensbrück to supervise the women's barracks, formally under the auspices of the Jewish women. On Christmas Eve, most of these women, who were former prostitutes, had a big party where all the German male prisoners had been invited. Especially intoxicated after the selection, the SS raided their gathering which soon turned into an orgy. After being severely beaten, the former prostitutes were soon sent back to Ravensbrück.

I later learned that each year at Dachau and other camps Christmas was also celebrated, but differently. At Dachau, Sturmer was in the habit of releasing a couple of dozen communists from the camp. He brought them to Nuremberg where they were ritualistically wined and dined as "repentant racial comrades". The most significant of these extensive discharges occurred on

Hitler's birthday in 1939, when roughly twenty-three thousand inmates from Buchenwald, this time mainly asocials, were relinquished. Discharged, they were required to sign a certificate pledging complete silence regarding all aspects of camp life. I then began to understand how Father as a German had always given so much importance to Christmas. However, he was no longer there to dress up like Santa Claus and come down the chimney. Instead, it was us, Jews, who were going up the same chimney.

Up to then, it was usually Abrasha who had been sent on the worst labor details, but later, in the winter, it was my turn. Why was I chosen and not another of those alleged intellectuals, who like my brother wore tortoiseshell rimmed glasses? Who knows. The only answer—Nazi arbitrariness. I was sent alone, without Abrasha, to Dundaga, one of the satellite camps of Kaiserwald, more than twelve miles inland from the Baltic Sea. There we lived like nomads in plywood tents, each night falling asleep to the merciless baying of the bloodhounds. The winter of 1943-1944 in Kurland had been one of the bitterest, where temperatures for the most part had hovered at minus twenty-five degrees Celsius. *Kommandant* Kröschl sent daily detachments of us in open vans to the sea. There we were forced to wade in the freezing water until it came up to our shoulders and then punch holes in the ice and slip in the corpses which we had brought with us. By April, the dead bodies had emerged. With the exception of myself and a few others, Kröschl's successor, Gustav Sorge, nicknamed Iron Gustav, a former professional thief, created a special *Kommando*, named the "Bathing *Kommando*", mainly comprised of so-called *Muselmänner*[26], emaciated creatures who had lost their strength, their hope and sometimes even their memories but who lingered on thanks to some survival instinct, what Freud would describe as *selbsterhaltungstreib* or

---

26 *Muselmann* (Muslim) was the camp slang for an inmate who had given up and was on the verge of death.

Über-Lebenstrieb, "instinct of self-preservation" or "life instinct", motivating them in this case to search for food. Ironically, others even volunteered for this *Kommando*, imagining that they would work in a warm bathhouse. On the contrary, we found ourselves placing the emerged corpses on pyres and igniting them with gasoline. The two months I spent there before returning to Kaiserwald impaired me psychologically for life. Like Abrasha, I was no longer the same. Never would I ever be the same. I too had become tempted by suicide but was somewhere too afraid of the consequences, should I fail.

While I was dredging bodies from the sea and burning them on pyres, Passover came and went. When on the beach, I could not help but reminisce with the others that in April only three years before, though we were under Russian rule, we as a family were at least still united. I closed my eyes and remembered so well the last Passover we had spent together with the exception, of course, of Father. All of a sudden, I imagined myself once again at my grandparents' house at the traditional gathering at the *Passover* supper, known as *seder*. During this eight day period which marked the beginning of Israel, to me probably the most moving of the holidays, my grandfather sat at the head of the table and would unroll the *Haggada*, from which he read to us proudly the story of the exodus of the Jews from Egypt, led by Moses. As I listened attentively, I sat with my cousins on one side of my grandparents' long wooden table, while my mother was seated on the other side and joined by some of our other relatives. Each of us children had our own colorful drinking cup with a tiny handle enough for our fingers to slip through. Near the table was the piano, clustered with many photographs of all the family. These pictures were so reassuring to me because they had always acted as a testimonial of our closeness. I suppose in some ways my former life had been what you might call a fairy tale, or so it seemed by comparison.

> *Mr. Schwabe, never forget that the love and stability that your family provided you with as a young boy has given you the force to combat the adversity with which you were confronted in the camps and throughout the rest of your life.*

Otherwise, I learned from Zenta, who had currently been transferred to a work detail in the airfield, that in April around four to five thousand Hungarian young girls and women had arrived. She said they looked and seemed even more pathetic than those at Kaiserwald. Appearing like scarecrows, they were hairless and wore long dresses that hung down to the ground. They all had been separated from their families, and according to my girlfriend were, not surprisingly, in a state of complete despair. Zenta told me how helpless she felt given that she had found no way to console them. Not long afterwards, she was also terrified when she realized that several trucks soon arrived, each time taking five hundred of them away until none were left. Whenever we met she repeatedly told me that she felt sooner or later we were all slated for the same fate. As time went on, things seemed to be going from bad to worse, so I could only agree with her.

Back in Kaiserwald it was late July. I looked across the barbed wire; I could see there was a selection in the women's camp. I quickly realized it was a *Kinderaktion*[27]. This was always the most heart-rending occurrence. SS Medic Wisner, the camp medic, together with Sauer, drove up in Wisner's small black sports car to initiate the event. Usually, the presiding doctor, often Krebsbach, was driven in the SS vehicle marked with a red cross, but not Wisner, who always preferred his creature comforts. Within a short period of time, he was ordering the sobbing children to the left or to the

---

27 A selection of children for mass killing and deportation.

right. The mothers were shrieking in the distance, some groveling at the feet of the SS, begging them hopelessly that either their sons or daughters could remain with them or if not, at least, allow them to accompany their children to their deaths. Requests of such kind were systematically refused because part of the pleasure of the ordeal was the satisfaction for the SS of having broken up a family. Otherwise, I could hear many of the mothers screeching out their children's names forlornly over the voices of the bellowing guards and the whelping dogs. Suddenly, I heard my mother's voice crying out hysterically. Had my sister been chosen? No, she was hollering out Rebecca's name instead. This time, even with Rebecca's stuffed breasts in an attempt to look older, she was unable to fool those bastards and to escape the cruel injustice of her destiny. Had she been only two years older, fourteen, she might have still been with us also to tell her story.

By now it had become almost certain that the war might be soon over since we heard incessantly the rolling thunder of heavy artillery in the distance. When we left in the morning for work, cars and trucks passed us by with household furniture in between the marching soldiers and civilians, all trying to rescue their possessions before the anticipated arrival of the Russian army. Was it not *déjà vu*? Had we not already witnessed this spectacle once in 1940 and again in 1941? When would it end?

A few hours later, another *Aktion* was held in the men's camp. It was late in the afternoon. I remember it like yesterday. A light summer rain began. Again, Wisner and Sauer appeared, but this time accompanied by Dr. Krebsbach. One thousand five hundred men and been chosen, including Abrasha and myself; selections always occurred in round numbers. As Wisner was reputed as a womanizer of the first order, this one was obviously less appealing to him than those involving the opposite sex. He also preferred the *Aktions* in the satellite camps where the inmates, the women in particular, were examined without clothes.

Despite the weather we were first ordered to run across the square, to demonstrate our level of physical fitness. While we were exhibiting our physical prowess or lack thereof, Wisner and the others were helping themselves to the liquor, the vodka and schnapps provided for them and contained in a nearby vehicle. Other guards, *kapos*, and SS, both Germans and Latvians, the latter the most dreaded, were also milling around. Many of them had been bought off by a liter of schnapps, a few cigarettes, or a hundred grams of bread and sausage. For them it was certainly worthwhile—some food and drink against a few Jewish lives. Why not?

Having seemingly passed the first test, Abrasha and I lined up to undergo the last inspection. This was my fifth and Abrasha's seventh selection. Despite this, each was admittedly as traumatic as the next. Except for very blatant cases, no one could really predict the outcome; much depended on the mood and the state of intoxication of the doctors. Anyway, we always tried to look our best and whenever possible to stand in the last row in order to be less visible. Abrasha as usual walked ahead of me, given he was the older. This was probably part of a tacit understanding between us. All of a sudden, to my utter consternation, Wisner, while joking drunkenly with Krebsbach, told Abrasha to "Come here!". He motioned him emphatically with his head, as was his custom, to the right where some of the other men were already standing. Why my brother and not I? This was the first of many questions that went through my mind. Only after the war did I understand that an individual who wore glasses was equated with the middle class, often professionals or intellectuals who had derided the Nazis. They were even nicknamed *Brillenschlange* (verbatim: eyeglass snake, actually cobra). The worst offenders were men like my brother, who wore tortoiseshell glasses, considered the ultimate confirmation of middle class or even upper class status.

As it became dark, I walked on, numbed with fear and shock. I kept looking back helplessly, tears running down my eyes. What could I do? How could I save my brother? Why should I live and not he? Only an hour later, we could hear, close by, the Nazis accompanied by their bloodhounds, screeching as they whipped the first fifty doomed men into a foreboding dark truck. The next day, devastated, I went to the barbed wire fence and told Mother. I need say no more, she was destroyed.

With the arrival of the Russians on Latvian soil, the first group of inmates in early August were marched to the Riga docks and loaded onto boats for the Stutthof Concentration Camp via Danzig. We were loaded like swine into the vessel, *Bremerhafen*. In all we were eight thousand men and nine hundred women, only three hundred of the men and five hundred of the women survived; sixty of them also died immediately after liberation. Additionally, there were also three thousand Hungarian Jewish women who had arrived in Riga via Auschwitz as well as three thousand prisoners of war. Afterwards, the second and last transport of Jews including my mother, Svetlana, and Zenta would leave at the end of September on the eve of *Yom Kippur*; Riga was then entirely *judenrein*, cleansed of Jews, before the arrival of the Russians in mid-October.

Once on the ship, we were trapped mercilessly in the hold, now also under the auspices of a crew of Austrian soldiers who were undoubtedly as anti-Semitic as the Latvians, if that could even be imagined. As we cruised along to our future destination, Russian flyers came and bombed three nearby ships, one carrying ammunition, one supplies, and still another German soldiers. All sank. Many anticipated that our ship would be the next to be fired upon. We were given no water or food. In the heat of August, our thirst was excruciating, creating an epidemic of coughing, even gagging. Many of us thought that we would choke. Finally, at one point the crew deigned to give us some water by having a high pressure hose sprayed upon us. Yet, generally if anyone wanted to get a little water for himself, he was hit over the head with a rifle butt. We furthermore became seasick, vomiting over each other. There were also no latrines so we used buckets instead which we hoisted up to the deck in order that our excrement could be thrown overboard.

After two days, those among us who survived finally arrived in Danzig, twenty-one miles outside of Stutthof. Most of us were not surprisingly in a state of total exhaustion. No one really understood where we were, nor where we were going. Guarded at bayonet-point, we were herded onto a large meadow, where each of us at last was given a small loaf of bread. There were also several places where water was finally available from large pitchers. The men and the women were separated by a smaller meadow, but within a distance where they could still talk with one another. Thank God.

In the evening, we were ordered into several barges which were usually used to ship sand and rocks up and down the Vistula. Five hundred of us were crammed upon each vehicle, which was probably best equipped to fit a hundred at most. The numerous barges were connected by chains and we finally left Danzig when, around midnight, a tugboat arrived to pull us out of the harbor. Once again, we were ordered to remain in the hold, under very much the same conditions as our earlier journey, except this time we were forced to stand up for all of the trip, making matters even worse. At one point, I miraculously maneuvered my way to the deck, where the scene was completely operatic. While the full moon was shining in the sky, its light mirrored a multitude of reflections in the water. Visible, too, were the silhouettes of the barges while we listened to the relentless cry of the seagulls. As we moved lazily along, the water lapped incessantly against the sides of the boats as we passed under the drawbridge. One woman wrapped in a grey blanket was standing upon the deck, wailing deliriously. Was she not on stage? But which stage? Could she be an actress in hell?

In the meantime, as the sun came up, we passed the cattle grazing on the shore and the mares with their foals scampering near the grayish-white wooden farmhouses. By now I was sure that we must have passed the border. Not only were the roads well paved, but I saw, chugging arrogantly along, a large number of black locomotives on which were written in an imposing script: "*Räder Rollen für den Sieg*" (Wheels are Turning for Victory); they acted, in fact, as gigantic symbols of the Nazis never-ending war effort. Otherwise, there were children impeccably dressed, the boys in shorts, held up by suspenders and the girls with their long braids in neatly pressed pinafores, waiting patiently at the crossings for our endless caravan to pass. *Doctor, they looked like characters on a billboard promoting Germany.* The surroundings were also full of military personnel; some waiting to catch trains and others taking care of their wounded. As we approached closer to our destination, we saw men in prison garb along the shore; they held up their picks in friendly salutation.

STUTTHOF

We finally reached Stutthof. As of 1940 it was originally a concentration camp mainly for delinquent or politically active Poles; however, with the reduction of the frontline as well as an excess of prisoners at Auschwitz and other camps, it was quickly converted into an extermination camp. In 1944, a separate section for Jews was added as well as a sickbay, gas chamber and crematorium. It was initially under the jurisdiction of Danzig's local government, until Himmler's visit at the end of 1941, when shortly after he ordered the camp to be enlarged and to become a state concentration camp. While Stutthof had been the first concentration camp created outside of the Reich's borders, the first pure extermination camp was Chelmno/Kulmhof in reclaimed German territory, followed by Belzec, Sobibór and Treblinka. There, mainly Jews were killed, but also gypsies, typhus victims, Soviet POWs and the insane. There was a sign attached to a van on which was inscribed "To the Bath". The inmates having been ordered to shower while their clothes were being disinfected found themselves gassed, once having climbed the ramp leading into the truck. Otherwise, extermination camp or not, what one must also keep in mind is Germany's love of camps. No, not just concentration camps designed to do away with us, Jews, but all sorts of camps... War camps, sports camps, Hitler Youth camps, summer camps, rest camps, political convention camps, the Reich's civil service camps, repatriate camps, war refugee and exile camps, bombed village camps, transitional and placement camps, intern camps, prisoner of war camps and a plethora of others. Why? Maybe, it was another means by which the Nazis believed they could better control society through its systematization. But that's once again only a guess.

In any case, until the SS arrived during the latter part of 1939 with a few hundred inmates sentenced to die, Stutthof had been inhabited only by the dullest of Europeans, the Prussian Germans, whose only pleasure when not berry-picking nor searching for mushrooms was cups and ale. Ironically, Stutthof since ancient times was also called the Forest of the Gods, as according to folklore, many centuries ago gods were alleged to have lived among its slender, elongated pines... not German gods, not Odin, nor Thor, but Lithuanian gods. Were they not since chased out by the devil?

We slowly approached, in rows of five, an imposing intricately sculptured white metal gate topped with a replica of a medieval turret on which Stutthof was spelled out in very large letters; spanning its entire width was also the inscription "*Arbeit macht frei*" (work makes you free). The initial shock of entering a new camp was always considered the worst. It was consequently then when the death rate was the highest. At first glance, however, Stutthof resembled more a resort than a concentration camp. In front, close to the watchtower, stood the red brick- two-story administrative building with Nazi flags, which looked more like a three or four star hotel than camp headquarters. Nearby, there were also numerous immaculate white houses with green shutters surrounded by flowers to house the SS, while further behind wooden barracks existed for the inmates, all painted in a dismal grey. As we passed with trepidation through the gate, the surrounding landscape was perfectly manicured, reflecting once again the habitual sense of Teutonic order and neatness. The grounds comprised a miniature garden in which peacocks strutted, and included a pond and swan house, answering to the Nazi's sense of esthetics.

Although upon admission, a selection was often held, for whatever reason we were spared this ordeal. Yet, we were accosted by German SS, Ukrainian guards, and by a bevy of Polish-Aryan *kapos* in blue berets and prison clothes. Most of them carried a short whip hidden up their sleeves with which, while screaming, they beat us ferociously. Simultaneously, buckets were passed around in which we were told to deposit our remaining valuables, yet most of us had little left to relinquish. Of our few remaining treasures, as usual, it was the women who were the cleverest at hiding them, sometimes in the ground, in latrines, or even in their vaginas.

While, we, the Latvian Jews had already been completely cleaned out at Kaiserwald, the Lithuanian Jews were delivered directly to the camp from the Siauliai and Kaunas ghettos, having been ordered to bring with them their most valuable possessions, be it gold, diamonds, furs or whatever else. Some of the inmates were given an apomorphine injection, to create vomiting, if for one reason or another it was suspected that an important valuable had been swallowed. Many of the SS, as at Kaiserwald, helped themselves to any item which could further enrich them. *Rapportführer* Arno Chemnitz, the equivalent of a major sergeant and a confirmed Nazi had since his adolescence even organized an illegal jewelry workshop placed under the auspices of *Oberkapo* Fritz Selonke, the camp's second executioner and second senior, a former butcher and bank robber. Skilled workmen were clandestinely employed there and produced all sorts of gold memorabilia including the gold "*Hitler Jugend*" badges, which were very much in vogue in camp. Allegedly, by the winter of 1945, Chemnitz, Selonke, and many other SS were millionaires if not billionaires. Furthermore, when the wealthy transports arrived, the camp administration ordered that sewage ditches be dug by the bath. Groups of SS officers marched up to their chests through the sewers in overalls, in search of any Jewish treasures. Sooner or later some of the stolen valuables would end up in the "Persian bazaar", having been organized by some of the prisoners where everything and anything was traded that the inmates had managed to keep away from the authorities.

Otherwise, on that scorching August day, we spent hours on the grounds where Master Sergeant Lüdtke, son of a businessman from Danzig and one of the camp's notorious sadists, organized one of his favorite pastimes, a gymnastic exhibition to humiliate us. There, we were forced to squat, stretch our hands out forward and leap across the entire camp yard like frogs. Later, some of my other Jewish campmates related their initial experiences which were equally debasing.

A few who had arrived on the earlier transports described some of the tortures which they underwent. A sawhorse used for carpentry was placed on the grounds, and once one of the Jews had bent over and taken down his pants, he, for instance, was beaten gleefully to a pulp by the SS. Others reported to us that when they arrived they had to fall to the ground and kiss it; this was followed by the Nazi – organized "welcome". There, the Jews had to shake hands, and after were ordered to beat each other with their fists. They were then ordered to hit each other with shovels.

They also told us that after the Jews, the clergy, at least initially, were among the camp's pariahs and were often even housed with the Jews. Why the priests? Possibly because they preached another religion other than Nazism. For the Jewish newcomers, there were also apparently other tortures that both they and the priests were forced to endure together. For example, they were ordered to lie down on the ground, while some of the clergy walked over the Jews and vise versa. The Jews were also coerced to kiss the clergy and be photographed.

Anyway, at the end of this endless afternoon came *Entlausung* (delousing), but when we saw the sign BATHHOUSE in large bold letters, there was a moment of panic, because rumor had it that the bathhouse, like at Chelmno/Kulmhof and other camps was actually a gas chamber. There, however, we were told to enter naked except for our shoes, in which some had sewn their valuables. Strangely enough, other transports were allowed to keep only their belts, still others only a razor, shaving soap, and shaving brush, sometimes also a spoon, sometimes not. As usual, the Nazis had an unfathomable sense of logic. Then, too, our hair was shaved off in a broad stripe about three centimeters wide across the top of our heads with a razor, not dissimilar to a knife used for cutting ducklings; the Germans referring to this band as "the road of lice". By now, in fact, colonies of lice were discovered whenever our hair grew back and consequently had to be cut all over again. Otherwise, we were inspected so thoroughly that even the men's anuses and the women's vaginas were examined should someone have hidden one of his remaining possessions.

After having been once again pulverized and harassed, the *kapos* pushed the handle of their whips into our anuses, allegedly to further disinfect us, but mainly once again to denigrate us. Then, we were issued a suit of prison cotton underwear, a shabby pullover, a striped bluish-grey prison suit also in cotton, a striped KZ beret and wooden clogs in place of shoes. Towards evening, we were registered. We had to state what kind of work we did and to which transport we belonged. Additionally, we had to specify whether we were of Aryan or non-Aryan descent. Afterwards, we were given our new prison numbers, printed on a white piece of cotton, with the six-pointed yellow Star of David outlined in black next to the number, which we wore on the left side of our chest; at Auschwitz, the inmates' identification numbers were tattooed unto their arms.

Otherwise, the political inmates, as at Kaiserwald, sported a red triangle next to their number. After, the professional criminals, who wore green stars, they were also the best adapted to camp life because they, too, unlike ourselves, had been the most psychologically prepared and expected the worse. Interestingly, those carrying the red triangle were also extremely numerous because it seemed that when the Nazis were uncertain of how to classify a prisoner, they, for whatever reason, determined him a political prisoner. Not only the clergy but even the infants and newborns were, in their twisted minds, classified as political inmates and were given the red triangle.

> *I suppose it was next to impossible to categorize a baby as a homosexual, a prostitute, or even a criminal. You agree with that, Doctor, don't you ?*

Anyway, there was one and practically only one type of prisoner who was released from camp, those who had been imprisoned for discipline or reform. In fact, during the camp's existence, there were roughly eight thousand of these inmates released, but all gained their freedom only under certain conditions: that they signed a form handed out by the Political Division stating that all their belongings had been restored, that they never suffered from either disease or mutilations, that they promised never to discuss what they saw, heard or endured while in camp, that once they would regain their liberty, should they hear somebody either working or speaking against the National Socialists, they would promise to inform the police, and lastly that this document was signed at the prisoner's free will and not under force.

Later, we were assigned to blocks and in keeping with my usual good fortune, I was assigned to one supervised by the dreaded Wacek Kozlowski, a Pole from the coastline who was formerly a butcher and who was reputed to have killed his own brother after arriving at camp. Beginning in 1944, like the other camp authorities, Kozlowski was forced to sign a document stating his cognizance that beating was completely forbidden; yet, this in no way arrested his violent and sadistic behavior. When he was not clobbering us, he was walking over us as he flailed his stick at us or he stood over us Jews, as we were prostrate on the ground and threw rocks and bricks at us. More grotesque and as was the tradition at Kaiserwald and other camps, following his brutal treatment, we were forced to thank him for his beatings and barbarity.

I came to believe that I was living in a world which had been turned completely upside down. Doctor, reassure me, any man would become crazy!

Additionally, we were made to leap again like frogs which always inspired in him infinite joy. If not, we were forced to squat on one leg like fakirs, or crawl on our bellies like lizards across the sandy yard. However, Wacek's specialty was execution, which he was always unable to resist. I was told by my bunk mates that earlier in the spring of 1944, the camp authorities were ordered by the *Gestapo* to hang a Polish girl. This was the first execution of a female in camp and even the German executioners got cold feet and refused to hang her. Wacek, of course, full of enthusiasm, took care of the job without any qualms, setting the precedent in camp for the future executions when women should again stray too far off the beaten track.

In my block, which was equipped to hold between three to four hundred men, we were over a thousand. As all the other barracks, ours was made of wood from the trees cut down by the inmates. We slept on three-tiered beds covered with straw. While three slept on the upper and middle tier, four now slept on the lower, all amidst the lice and the bed bugs, which we chased with a candle, even leaving stains on the wall. At Dachau, apparently it was even worse because there existed what the prisoners called "dog cells"; one of my block mates told me that they had had to lie on one side of the bunk and to bark like dogs while their food was passed. We were also informed by our supervisors that we should consider ourselves very fortunate in comparison to the prisoners at Salaspils who, while the camp was being built, slept outside, even in winter, without either pillows or mattresses. One must realize everything is relative. Anyway, when we were too overcrowded, some slept on the floor of the barracks. When the toilets in our barracks were stopped up, the Aryan blocks, mainly Polish, did not allow us, Jews, to use their latrines. When they did find one of us in the toilets, they beat us to a pulp. It was then I realized how anti-

Semitic they were. Though until this day, I really don't know why the Poles hated us so much.

Anyway, our days resembled in many ways those at Kaiserwald, only worse, mainly because now at all times, death seemed right around the corner. We were awakened to the sound of a bugle and the screaming of the *kapos*, at five in the morning. *Heraus! Heraus! Appell! Appell!* Now, we were herded to a large space, referred to as the parade grounds, where we were counted and recounted in the morning and again at night; this sometimes lasted as much as three to four hours. The only inmates spared this ritual were the convicts that worked in the building containing the gas chamber and crematorium, of which I would later become one. Last but not least, regarding the food, again we were being starved to death. In the morning, we were given watery coffee and a slice of bread, for lunch, a quart of so called soup, made of turnips and turnip tops, and for supper a slice of bread, and a dot of margarine; finally, every Saturday, a slice of sausage and Sunday a tiny piece of cheese. Was this not their gesture of *noblesse oblige*?

Almost immediately upon arrival, I was also very upset to find the inmates who had already been imprisoned at Stutthof for a period of time were jealous of us newcomers. Why? Because of our virility. They thought that we had had sex more recently than they did. Actually, at Kaiserwald we did have access to the opposite sex on Sundays, where here, effectively, we had none. Consequently, in order to completely destabilize us, they lied to us, pretending that they had been castrated. No one could believe my state when I heard this. Some were asking where the operation would take place and how much it hurt. We soon realized that this was pure fabrication, but it really does not speak well for human nature. Didn't Shakespeare always tell us to be aware of the green-eyed monster[28]?

---

28 "O, beware my lord, of jealousy;/It is the green-eyed monster which doth mock/The moth it feeds on" Extract from *Othello*

Anyway, Doctor, I am sure this is a problem that you must be up against every day.

I also need to tell you that I was in a particularly vulnerable period given that Abrasha's death had just occurred a few weeks earlier. I felt completely alone and unprotected. All the women in my life were still at Kaiserwald or so I hoped. I seriously questioned if they too would not be selected, particularly Mother and Svetlana, given that Mother was over forty and Svetlana, only thirteen. I was less worried about Zenta who was older and thus less likely to be chosen. I also wondered if they and the others remaining at Kaiserwald were to be sent here, or somewhere else.

During this phase of total anxiety, I must confess, I had a very brief homosexual experience, which of course was counter to everything both my religion and my education had taught me. Homosexuality, for a Jew, was the ultimate sin. I still feel guilty about it today, but I must admit that it temporarily strengthened me, because I realized that I was not impotent. It also made me feel if not loved, at least wanted. Now, I have learned to no longer hate myself for it. But I still prefer not to speak about it. I am happy too that neither Father nor Abrasha ever learned about it. I fear they might have no longer considered me a man, but then again maybe they would have realized it was an act of desperation.

In any case, even if I prefer to avoid it now, some day I know I must tell you more about it. But I hope, Doctor, that you will never hold it against me.

Of course not, Mr. Schwabe.

During this period of particular fragility, I was especially sensitive to my behavior, as well as the comportment of others. I was amazed, for example, how many of the inmates, yes, the Jewish inmates, really aped the SS. Although, it was already apparent at Kaiserwald, now it seemed even more flagrant. Maybe because the prisoners had been there longer? The Jewish men in my barrack did everything and anything they could to become the carbon copy of the SS. They not only adopted the same goals, values and attitudes, but they even tried to look like them. Whenever the inmates could find some part of an SS uniform, the Jews would even sew it on to their own prison wear. Actually, they were often punished for it, but this did not deter them. They told us they wanted to look "smart", so as to resemble the SS, whom they equated with power. They also prided themselves if during roll call they had stood well and or saluted well; they were constantly searching the officers' approval in one way or another.

Finally, the Jews often also replicated the sadistic leisure activities of the SS. One of the preferred games of the officers was to find out who could stand being hit for the longest period of time without screaming out in resistance. Additionally, the inmates prided themselves on being as tough or tougher than the SS. I was sickened and alarmed to learn to what extent my fellow barrack mates had been brainwashed and manipulated over time by these odious Germans.

In any case, not even a week after entering Stutthof, a group of Polish Jews arrived at camp, some of whom were lodged in our overcrowded block. They recounted their seemingly interminable journey in cattle cars. One of the Poles, whose first name was Avrom but whose last name escapes me, had been a former professor and politician. Like Abrasha, he, too, wore glasses, a *Brillenschlange* and had miraculously evaded a selection at Auschwitz under the auspices of the infamous Mengele. He told me about their horrifying voyage in cattle cars where they were packed like sardines for a couple of days without either water or food and in which his brother died, among quite a few others. The car apparently had only two small windows located at the top of the wall on either side, which was unreachable and covered on the outside by barbed wire. In the car, there was loose straw covering the floor and standing in one corner, there was a big bucket, which served as the toilet. In the meantime, they urinated through the splits in the opening of the wooden floor. However, at the end of the train, there was a caboose car for the guards whom he imagined were inevitably comfortably installed and as usual well fed.

He was further repelled by the guards who had placed him under a twelve hour initiation period; for some, it had been even longer. Like myself, he had been forced to hit his fellow Jews and furthermore vilify his value system by charging the others of heinous acts; he was forced to accuse the women in his family, for instance, of prostitution and adultery. Until it ended, as was always the case, anyone who had not obeyed one of the commands issued to him such as beating another prisoner or assisting in the torture of another inmate was accused of mutiny and punished by death.

We soon spoke often together and quickly bonded. Probably, one of the reasons we were especially drawn to each other was the fact that we had both so recently lost our brothers. Avrom in some way also resembled Father, in the sense that he too seemed to know so much, to be so well informed. From him, I therefore learned a lot. Among many topics, he spoke to me particularly about politics. I understood from him that the laws against the Jews which had been created by the Vichy government were surprisingly much more severe than the Nuremberg edicts. He also informed me that the deportation of the Jewish children was an initiative often undertaken by the French, not the Germans, as one might have expected. In any case, Avrom believed that some of the French were among Germany's greatest collaborators. He also recounted that Denmark and Bulgaria were the two countries where the Jews had been the best treated. Many of the Danish Jews with the aid of their government were smuggled to neutral Sweden. Albeit the Bulgarian Jews were dispossessed of their property and forced to live outside of the capital, they were still not deported and sent to concentration camps, like we, the poor Latvian Jews. Avrom asserted that this was due to the fact that neither of these countries had ever been subject to severe anti-Semitism and also because most of the Bulgarian and Danish political leaders refused to be influenced by Nazi propaganda.

He also apprised me of one Hillel Storch, a Swedish Jew of Latvian descent, who was to become the head of the Swedish section of the World Jewish Congress, and with the help of Doctor Felix Kersten, was aiding the Jews to a maximum. Kersten was Himmler's doctor to whom he was completely indebted for having relieved his uncontrollable stomach pains through massage.

In fact, I questioned whether or not his illness was not psychosomatic. What do you think, Doctor? Himmler, for me, was a perfect candidate for a psychosomatic disorder.

He must, at some level, have been riddled with guilt. In any case, Kersten used his power over him to save any and every possible life he could. With Storch, he also set up a program which sent food and medical supplies to the camps, gave a maximum amount of aid to the Jews in the camps through the intervention of the International Red Cross, helped the release of individual prisoners whenever possible and tried to transfer many Jews to Sweden and Switzerland. Maybe, after all, Doctor Kersten should have also accepted to care for Hitler. Might he not have had the same power over the Führer? Maybe, he could have managed to spare hundreds of other lives, or maybe more ?

We spoke, too, about life in the camps which was really a subculture onto itself. The prisoners had, if not their own language, at least their own slang, consisting of words such as "*Nachschlag*", receiving additional food, "*Scheisshaus*", toilet or other ones such as "*Muselmann*" or "delousing", only to mention a few. We both realized that given we were subject to so much suffering, it was often difficult to separate daydreams from reality. At times we also both endured lapses of memory, in fact, I am still today often faced with this problem.

This is completely habitual, Mr. Schwabe.

Similar to the other prisoners, our conversations were often related to the brutality of camp life, if not, we exchanged rumors or speculated about our potential liberation. We were also aware of the necessity of bonding and the impossibility of confronting camp life alone. However, the Nazis were aware of this and fearful that any unity among the inmates could result in some form of rebellion or at worst, insurrection such as the uprising in the Warsaw Ghetto in 1943. Thus, prisoners were separated by moving them from time to time to another barrack or another work detail, while others were even transferred to a different camp. In fact, Avrom believed that this was the reason that he had been sent to Stutthof. In any case, we agreed that the ultimate goal of the SS was to break us of our individuality in order that we were impotent to resist them. Amazingly, the fear of punishment was furthermore often more traumatic than the act, itself. What we additionally remarked upon was if we had received some form of minimal punishment, such as being slapped, we tended to be ashamed of it and sometimes even denied it. Why did we prefer, for instance, to be whipped? Simple. If the suffering was great, we still felt in possession of our manhood.

It all got back to that. If it was minor, we felt as if we being treated as children which to us was even more degrading. Doctor, does it surprise you?

In my profession, nothing surprises me.

As for me, the more I think about it, the more I realize to what degree of inhumanity we had been reduced.

While we, the Jews, as well as almost all the other prisoners, were morally shattered by the authorities, there was one group and only one who seemed to remain almost impervious, the purple triangles, the Jehovah's Witnesses. It was the *Bibelforscher*[29], who treated, to the amazement of ourselves and the other prisoners, the SS and the others in charge with equanimity. At Stutthof, they were mainly part of a rather peaceful protestant denomination active in Eastern Prussia, Austria and Western Poland; while the majority of them were German, there were also some Poles. Although the Jehovah Witnesses were only a few dozen in the various camps, they still maintained high visibility. They recognized absolutely no spiritual hierarchy, everyone was equal. They worked in the houses of the SS and were trusted by them as well as by most of the inmates. In any case, the Jehovah's Witnesses were not only Christians, but also pacifists which were among the major reasons for their incarceration. Furthermore, in the initial questionnaire they were required to fill out when entering camp, they proudly and defiantly signed "Jehovah's Witness". Likewise, when many were told that should they affirm in writing the renunciation of their religion, they would be immediately released, the Jehovah's Witnesses systematically refused. Until this day, I can still remember the ruler of the women's barracks, the garrulous, husky looking shrew, *Frau* Belenke, screaming at the top of her lungs at Traugott Mayer, the commander of the camp's prisoners:

"What right do you executioners have," she yelled, threatening Mayer with her manly fist, "to lock up people in camps and torture them?! You murderers, all of you Nazis, should go up the crematorium chimneys yourselves! I'm telling you, a day will come when you'll be sitting in my place. That day isn't far off! I'm not signing any of your lousy papers! I'll wait for the day

---

29 The Jehovah's Witnesses.

when you executioners all hang. I'll leave this place then without signing a thing!"[30]

Mayer and the other Nazis were angered by the ungovernability of *Frau* Belenke and the other Jehovah's Witnesses; however, they also seemed incapable of any form of retaliation. It was always *Frau* Belenke and her followers who with refractoriness had the last word, and who always remained unscathed; it was they who seemed empowered, not, for once, the Nazis. Maybe we should have followed their example, but our instincts told us that since we were Jews and the main targets of the Germans, their reactions would never have been as indulgent.

It was soon the end of September and *Yom Kippur*, ten days after the Jewish New Year. I remembered when in the ghetto the last time we celebrated this holiday as a family and we tried to hold on to our remains of optimism. *Kol Nidre*, the prayer that opens the service, was recited in our poor homes which functioned as makeshift synagogues.

Simultaneously, I can also recollect how worried most of our fellow Jews had been by this time, regarding our future. To appease their angst, I remember how more than a few resorted to magic and spiritualism, finding no longer any solace in traditional religion. I could still hear, for instance, our neighbors frantically crying out in desperation while lifting a table:

"Speak, table, speak or rise, table, rise."

The table began to rise in the same way that many of their family members, particularly the very young and the very old had been lifted up by the SS and thrown into trucks.

"Rap, rap, rise table, rise! And let us know where are my little Leah, Sarah, and George.

Speak. Speak. Are they with Mother and Father?

Have the children found shelter and food?

Rap. Rap.

Do they miss us?

---

30 Balys Sruoga, *Forest of the Gods*, p. 231.

Speak. Speak.

Will we see them again? No.

Are they asleep forever? Rise, table, rise."

But the table no longer moved. Afterwards, our neighbors became silent. Then they wept.

Now, three years later, many more had completely lost faith including myself. Others, surprisingly, had not. David, one of my bunkmates, also a Jew from Riga, was a salient example. After reciting the *Kol Nidre* which marked the beginning of the twenty-five hour period of purification, he stood near our bunk, almost delirious with his eyes closed, swaying back and forth, his body even shaking with religious zeal. Given the life we had all been forced to undergo, it seemed so absurd that he, David, or the other Jews in the concentration camps should be asking God forgiveness for the sins they had committed within the last year. It seemed moreover that the Germans should be asking pardon, certainly not us. In any case, I heard David repeating with conviction over and over again "For the sins we have committed before Thee". Each time, he reiterated the same phrase in a manner almost trance-like. With his head raised up, his fists clenched, he fanatically hit his chest, while stamping his feet. He refused to understand that God had, in fact, abandoned us.

At the end of September, Mother, Svetlana, and Zenta arrived at camp. A few days after their entry into Stutthof, I found them standing fatalistically at the barbed wire. Despite the obstacles in communicating, little by little, I learned that their journey from Kaiserwald was very similar to my own. They confessed that at no point did they feel certain that they would survive. There was furthermore a selection upon their arrival and as usual they were very fearful that Svetlana and Mother would be chosen, but once again as they had so often done in the past, while Svetlana stuffed her breasts, they both stood in the back row and so managed to pass by unnoticed. After the ubiquitous delousing procedure, they were assigned to their barracks. This time, they were equally unfortunate. Zenta was sent to Block nineteen, one of the Jewish barracks, and placed under the supervision of Maks Musolf, a Polish *kapo* who was uncontestedly one of the most brutal overseers at Stutthof. It was rumored that he had already been imprisoned for eleven years for having assassinated both his wife and children. At camp, he was especially notorious for partaking in the initial selections, as well as for his "autographs" which accompanied his beatings; true to himself, children, then women, were among his favorite victims, many of whom, like his family, had already died from his blows. Zenta quickly learned that the only means to avoid his punishments was through paying him off with gold fillings, given his unquenchable rapacity. After the war, he was tried in Hamburg and was fortunately executed in the fall of 1946. After having battered my girlfriend to bits I was more than ecstatic to have been apprised of his justified demise. For once, somebody got what they deserved.

Doctor, don't consider my reactions vindictive; they are only human.

In the meantime, neither Mother nor Svetlana were blessed with a lucky star. They were sent to Blocks twenty-one and twenty-two, under the auspices of Elzinka and Bozka, respectively. They were Czech *kapos* along with their cousin Katia, who were self-hating Jews, who, striding along in their high black boots, treated the women with utmost cruelty, hitting them with horsewhips. Sometimes, they threatened also to have them gassed, screaming at them that they were not even worth the three *pfennige*, for the cost of a metal bullet. Allegedly, they had arrived from Bohemia, introduced by an eminent *Oberscharführer* whose name I have now forgotten. Thus, they were the women in charge, serving the SS, and thus both my mother and sister were totally powerless against them.

Otherwise, whether the men or the women were better or worse treated remains debatable. The women's death count was in relative terms supposed to be much lower than the men's. Except for the harvest in the spring when they worked in the open fields, some worked in the kitchen, some even in the kitchens of the SS, helping themselves whenever they were unobserved, to the best of the leftovers. Others also worked as governesses and maids for the SS officers or took care of the clothing where they were almost always able to "organize" an extra pair of underwear, or a shirt, or a dress which, if they did not keep them for themselves, could always be traded.

Zenta's arrival gave me great joy, but simultaneously equal frustration. In a word, we were perpetually separated by an electric barbed wire fence. Unlike Kaiserwald, physical encounters with the opposite sex were at all times forbidden and the guards even chased us away from the fence with whips. We gazed and consumed each other with our eyes and communicated with any type of sign language possible, as did rows of other lonely men and women glued to the barbed wire like flees. Sunday nights, following the afternoon concert, some of the Jewish inmates could no longer contain themselves and driven by love or lust, broke the fence when it was not electrically charged or else managed to dig under it. Some women crossed into the men's barrack and vice versa and were later found in each other's arms in some deserted workshop or washroom. Initially, both Zenta and I were too fearful of the eventual consequences of such a rendezvous, until one October night, love conquered all. Unfortunately, we were discovered near the women's barrack by one of the Ukrainian guards and turned into the authorities. Then came the inquisition, followed by the curses, shrieks, and tears, and ultimately the habitual punishment doled out to romantics such as ourselves. While some men were confined to the bunker for a few days, others such as myself were sent to the *Hopehill* brick factory, referred to as the abyss, for hard labor. All things being relative, I still found it almost better than my sojourn at Dundaga. Meanwhile, Zenta, along with the other women who had been caught, was punished and beaten.

Otherwise, Arno Chemnitz, the Nazi responsible for the inmates' punishments, decided to humiliate, or so he hoped, an adulterous couple who had also been discovered. The woman was married and in her fifties and the man was half her age and young enough to be her son. Chemnitz ordered the couple to hold hands and snuggle up to each other, while the camp members watched them walk around the parade grounds. Could they not have been in Hawthorne's New England instead of a concentration camp?

Afterwards, Zenta and I still corresponded by mail which was again another art unto itself. Our letters were transmitted by go-betweens, special couriers who were generally Russian. They were usually motivated enough to take the risk and in any case were masters at supporting any of the consequent lashings. Near the women's' barrack stood an enormous garbage container where the Russian intermediaries would pick up and deliver the letters. Whenever one of the guards would find one of the Russians in the garbage bin, they would throw him out with all sorts of threats, but soon afterwards another Russian would have quickly replaced him. These letters were later intercepted by the authorities. They were usually written in Polish or Russian and translated by the Nazis. Ours were written in German and therefore we were particularly careful about what we said.

Our superiors also indulged in romance and sex, but the Führer's laws did not contend equally with all the different races and nationalities. As an example, for sexual affairs with German women, only Russians and Poles were sent to concentration camps. Even the detested Jews were not always treated all in the same way. Otherwise, as you know, the authorities themselves were more often than not attracted to our Jewish women, even though sexual relations remained totally *verboten*. Although many of the SS were married they were also reputed for their rampant promiscuity. Just before my entrance into camp, the SS and other camp leaders were apparently overjoyed when earlier in the summer of 1944, a large group of Hungarian Jewesses crossed the camp's threshold and were hungry enough to have sex with them for even a crust of bread. Although Selonke, for example, was a chronic womanizer, he did not find it always convenient to visit the barracks of the Hungarian women. Consequently, in the evening, one of the Jewesses was delivered to him in the same box in which the bread was carried, and was systematically returned the next morning in the identical box.

In this same domain, the Ukrainian SS offered much unwanted competition to their German counterparts, by philandering systematically with the war widows in the town of Stutthof as well as the neighboring villages. To divert them, the authorities created facilities for the Ukrainians in camp. Small, cozy, romantic cottages were constructed in the pine grove and surrounded by barbed wire so the inmates would not be tempted to drop in and disturb them. Two of the most seductive young women, Niunce and Lola, were hand picked to service and entertain the few hundred sex starved Ukrainians. The brothel was run by Granny Krauss, a Prussian tramp who was one-eyed and bowlegged. In order to entice the soldiers, the camp authorities provided the two girls with all the amenities, be it silk stockings, garter belts, leather shoes, crepe de chine dresses, fur collars, variegated hats, powder, cream, cologne, and even dildos. However, the Ukrainians felt very short changed since their visits were limited to fifteen minutes and were no longer on the house. To make matters worse, the Ukrainians were no longer fed and were always thirsty since they were not even allowed a drop of alcohol.

As far as other recreation was concerned, there were also open-air concerts in the yard, but not as frequently as at Kaiserwald. A piano had been borrowed from one of the *kapo's* blocks and various and sundry instruments had been "organized" from the transports. Stupelis was considered one of the camp's uncontested stars, given in his former life he had been one of the leading violinists in the orchestra at the Kaunas Opera. Often a *Kirghiz*[31] danced, he was from some nomadic tribe. I was totally mesmerized by him as he kept performing in a trance-like state, even after the music stopped; dancing for him, I was told was part of his religion and some form of prayer. I envied his faith. Additionally, a group of professional Russian singers and dancers organized several performances, while the Poles arranged some variety shows under the auspices of Stephan Wronski-Majkowski, a director from Warsaw who was also particularly popular in camp. Meanwhile, the winter before my arrival, I was told that Selonke had also arranged a boxing match inside the camp store against one of the Polish professional boxers. The match was among the camps most important events, however everyone sympathized with the boxer, as he had absolutely no chance against Selonke.

> *How could he win against one of the camp's executioners? Camp life, Doctor, was a series of very lose–lose situations.*

In early November, during one of the bi-weekly or tri-weekly selections the few remaining children were slated for destruction. Mother, probably because she had children, herself, seemed particularly affected. She described to me the heart-rending scenario of a young boy, somewhere between eleven and twelve who very protectively looked after the younger children. At the time of the selection, the boy accompanied by his flock crawled on his belly to where the adults were standing; there, in order for all of them to

---

[31] The *Kirghiz* are Sunni Muslims from Central Asia.

look taller, he created a podium out of the sand for himself and the others to stand on. Yet, despite his efforts they were discovered almost immediately and were beaten and mercilessly herded into trucks, to the impatient screams of the guards.

It was also during this selection that I learned from Mother that Zenta had been among the women chosen to be sent to Sophienwalde, one of the many satellite camps. I was not surprisingly frozen with fear when I learned this news. Despite the fact that it was not our first separation, now for whatever reason, maybe by premonition, I felt a sense of loss and total powerlessness. I told Mother of my uncontrollable anxiety, who tried in turn to reassure me. Anyway, it was not until after the war that I was told that Zenta, at Sophienwalde, had been a roofer and had fallen off the top of a house and broken her neck and died. I was especially bereaved, given it seemed that liberation had been right around the corner.

I was also told by Luiza, my Polish friend who had also been at Sophienwalde, how the inmates there had been used for medical experiments. For instance, thirty-five women had been selected and put into a van where their moaning and groaning could be heard as they froze to death. Later, she learned, too, that the cadavers of the thirty-five women in question were delivered into the SS barrack where they were distributed among the seventy Latvian medical students for dissection, which explained why there were troughs on both sides of the stone floor of the buildings.

The Pole, Wlødzimierz Markuszewski who carried out the dissected bodies in large baskets soon went mad and for cause. Among the medical students was the red-haired, freckled faced Latvian SS, Vilis Kruze, who at Kaiserwald was already notorious for his mistreatment of us. After the war, he became even more infamous when employed by Kaiser-Permanente in Hawaii as a gynecologist; there, due to his incompetence he was responsible for the deaths of various women.

Soon after Zenta's transfer to Sophienwalde, there were also some changes in the camp supervisors of the Jewish division for women. While mainly German girls from the ages of twenty to thirty were brought in, Mother was blessed with one of the two older elephantine SS brought from Riga. This obese creature was an alcoholic who guzzled whiskey as if she was a truck driver and swore relentlessly at my mother and the other prisoners. Additionally, instead of beating them with clubs, she used narrow belts as she inflicted her perpetual punishments.

Concurrently, typhus had become rampant throughout Stutthof, and particularly in the barracks of the Jewish women. The epidemic was so overwhelming that it was necessary to close off the camp to the outside. By January, seventeen percent of the prisoners had died from it. The crematory could no longer handle the amount of dead bodies and burned down due to the oven's overload. Anyhow, the huge lice were omnipresent, the straw on the bunks had rotted and the lines outside the lavatories seemed to stretch for miles as the inmates were victims of the biting cold, despite the ever-glaring sun. Meanwhile, Svetlana had become gravely ill, her fever rising to 103°. But we all knew that should she be taken to the *Revier*, she had little to no chance of ever getting out. Despite the fact that she was so weak that she could barely walk and saw everything in a blur, Mother and two of her friends dragged her along, at least at first, to the laundry where they had been assigned to iron the shirts belonging to the SS; they sat her down next to them while they also did her work. However, she soon became so sick that the doctor selected her for the hospital. Then we were sure that we would never see her again. However, when a week later she had almost miraculously recovered, which was sometimes the case with the disease, she returned to the women's camp and confided to Mother her ghastly experiences.

In the hospital, the facility for the Jews was separated from the one that treated the Gentiles, yet this notwithstanding, both saw from their windows the gas chambers and the crematorium, despite the commands that the windows remain blinded.

As I was later to learn when I attended to the dead at camp, the gas chamber itself was built in 1943. The first year, it served only to disinfect the clothing. Afterwards, the inmates were originally gassed in small groups but the amount was quickly increased to about one hundred at a time. The prisoners, mainly Jewish men and women, were enclosed for roughly thirty minutes in the chambers; by this time they were dead as a consequence of having choked on *Zyklon B*. However, during the month of November, the gassing stopped, most probably in great part as a result of Himmler's general order to stop further extermination of the Jews, following his negotiations with numerous worldwide Jewish organizations.

At Stutthof, the Jewish women, almost inevitably, were also reputed for most often resisting the authorities. During the same year, one group of them revolted and unexpectedly pulled an SS into the gas chamber. Thus, the stationary chamber was substituted by two narrow-gauge cars, there being a side track near the crematory.

Afterwards, the SS created the "*Strumpfstopfen Kommando*", a stocking darners' *Kommando*. Some of the women skilled in darning stockings and knitting volunteered, while others were selected at morning roll call; given sewing and knitting needles, they were loaded into a railway car that was allegedly taking them to an area outside of Stutthof where they were to put their abilities to good use. The car itself was hitched either to a locomotive or to a goods train. When they arrived, a *Kommandant* adorned in a railway uniform told them with courtesy to please take the seat of their choice on the train. After the train had stopped at a station or two and the women screamed and raved, pounding hysterically on the doors, they shortly returned dead, having been killed by the gas. Wasn't this similar to so many of the ploys used by the SS as early as the ghetto,

Dünamünde among many? Before Svetlana was to come down with typhus, she tried everything in her power to convince Mother to volunteer along with herself for this *Kommando*. Given these same skills had once saved their lives, my sister again felt it was worth the gamble. But Mother's instincts fortunately told her otherwise.

Anyway, although the gassing had ended by now, and despite the fact that the windows of the *Revier* were supposed to be curtained, Svetlana could see the *Karren*, the transport wagons, dragging the inmates to the crematorium as well as hearing the helpless pleas of some of them who were still alive. She was also repelled that on a very regular basis she and the others had been fed glasses of urine rather than water. Furthermore, she was totally outraged by the abuse of the SS in the hospital. They staged a small selection in order to amuse and distract themselves, the women patients were ordered to undress and dance and prance in front of them. They laughingly made deriding jokes and then decided which ones were qualified for work or sexual exploitation, and which should be selected for the "final journey to Jerusalem". Whenever a woman was too emaciated or weak, with sheer delight they pointed a finger in the direction of the crematory and screamed out "*ins Krematorium*" (to the Crematorium!). The selection occurred at the end of Svetlana's sojourn, so she escaped the crematory. However, two of the SS forced her and a few others of her hospital mates into a drunken orgy. Svetlana still feels marred by this sexual abuse so many years later.

In any case, my life could have been best described as "shit". Why "shit"? After returning from *Hopehill*, I was arbitrarily given the assignment of what the clergy referred to as "*Scheisskolonne*", the work unit which cleaned out the latrines and the sewers. When, for instance, we were not assigned to the toilets, we were sent down, waist-deep into the sewers handing full buckets of excreta up to the clergy, in particular, which were afterwards emptied into vats or horse-drawn wagons. Otherwise, as a pastime the SS also drowned us, Jews, in ditches filled with liquid manure or in the latrine pits. After crawling in the camp's sewage ditches, and soaking wet with the excrement, we had to stand in the biting cold. Many of my comrades even froze to death and those who lived, unlike the SS, were never allowed to keep the odd treasures they found in the excrement. In any case, by early December an order came to supply five hundred workers from Stutthof for one of the neighboring camps. A group of us were sent to the parade grounds where we were ordered to jump over a box one meter high. As I wanted to remain with my mother and sister, I deliberately failed to negotiate the hurdle. Along with some others who had stumbled or touched it, I received a blow from the *kapo's* truncheons and was disqualified. Accompanied by the others who had also been unsuccessful in demonstrating their physical prowess, I was sent to Stutthof's beach and forced to lay in the sand until my eyes and mouth were filled with the sand blown by the brisk wind. Soon afterwards, we were made to act like a dog for the day. But why not? Had we not already played the part of other animals? In any case, the *kapos* walked by with a stick in their hands ordering us to sniff. Afterwards, they threw it as far as they could, commanding us to bark, run after the stick, and return it. When we brought it back to them, we received an inverted Pavlovian response, instead of a pat, we were given a blow. When they threw the stick the second time, it often landed near the electrified fence, so many of the inmates never returned.

Since it was just before Christmas, many of the Gentile inmates were waiting for news and perhaps even gifts from their families. SS Tech. Sergeant Platz, known in camp as The Bald Penguin, probably because of his receding hairline, became thus one of the camp's focal points, given he was the head postmaster. While before the war he had the honorary position of scraping horse droppings from the tramway tracks in Gdansk, now he had a sense of total empowerment, since he was in a position to snip off part of the inmates' correspondence whenever he had the pleasure of finding that it had exceeded the quota of lines allowed. Also, should some minute detail in any of the incoming or outgoing letters offend or even mildly disturb him, he immediately trashed them. When a prisoner was notified that a letter had arrived and he did not pick it up exactly at the minute or even the second designated by Platz, the prisoner was forced to abandon it. Otherwise, the SS block leader also occasionally appeared with a large packet of mail, reading off the names of the prisoners he had letters for. Soon afterwards, he would scream out: "Now you pigs, know you received mail" and proceeded to sadistically burn their long awaited correspondence. One day, just a week before Christmas, an SS appeared and told one of my bunkmates, without showing him the wire, that his brother had died. When the inmate asked which one of his three brothers was dead, the SS answered with disdain: "It's up to you to choose which one it should have been."

It was also just at this time that Mother after all these years miraculously received not a letter, but a clandestine brief note from Father. Although no Jews were allowed officially to receive mail, the note was given by Father to Gentile friends before they themselves were sent to Stutthof. He asked about the family and we were only happy that he knew nothing about Abrasha's death. Avoiding any of the ramifications, he alluded to his long and "difficult" imprisonment in justification of his silence. He wrote that through the help of some Gentile friends in Riga as well as some from the Germans, he was finally released and was able to track us down. We imagined like a dexterous puppeteer, Goebbels as usual in the end pulled the right strings. However, after the war, we were never able to locate Father so we could only imagine he was dead. It was only many years later, after my cousin, Joachim, found us in New York, that we finally learned what had happened to Father. Initially, he was arrested by the Germans, who suspected him of spying against them, but was finally released. Then, during his second arrest, under torture, Father admitted to work as a foreign agent for the C.I.A.. We learned that he had been hung in the beginning of 1945, with the benediction of his friend, Goebbels.

> *How did you feel, Mr. Schwabe, when you learned all of this?*
>
> *I felt complete horror! However, I was proud to also learn that my Father was a martyr, and I am still proud.*

Christmas finally came and with it the usual camp festivities. Traugott Mayer, the Bavarian commander of the camp's prisoners, had Stutthof decorated for the holidays, having ordered a huge fir tree in the middle of the parade grounds. It was situated not far from Himmler's Alley, the camp's main avenue, named, of course, after the undisputed lord of the concentration camps. Reminiscent of Kaiserwald and the Christmas Eve selection, while the multi-colored swastika lights were flickering next to the tree, Mayer had ordered gallows erected. In order to mark the coming of Christ, a bell sounded in order to summon the convicts to their execution; while their infractions were announced over the loudspeaker; the men were still dangling in the air a week later in further celebration of the New Year.

But generally, Mayer found that the hangings had become laborious, given that the camp had only one gallows tree and there were so many prisoners to execute. Consequently, while some were still hung, another procedure was created to kill the inmates with efficiency; one which was soon to become Mayer's favorite sport. It consisted of bringing them into a cubicle which vaguely resembled a phone booth, installed in a closed room which appeared to be a medical cabinet. In its back panel, the cubicle had an oblong slot. When an inmate was brought to the room, most of the time he was greeted by Arno Chemnitz. Dressed in a white lab coat,

Chemnitz pretended to give him a routine check up. Meanwhile, the prisoner was told to lean back against the slot and SS *Kommandant* of the Jewish camp, Ewald Foth, would shoot the victim in the back of the head, unless of course, he gave Mayer the pleasure to take his place. Otherwise, Foth was also reputed for giving the inmates a lethal injection, often of phenol in the heart. Meanwhile, the door to the crematory opened, and four inmates including later even myself would enter the room and collect the body.

In any case, one of the other popular techniques for liquidating us, Jews, were killing injections called "needlings". Otherwise, killer nurses led the victims to the bath under the pretense of washing them and there they would drown them by holding their heads under the water in the bathtub. Lastly, "bathing" was another type of killing process frequently practiced at the camp's hospital, the *Revier*. Naked patients were assembled in front of the bath in the freezing cold, then they would be showered alternatively with ice cold water and scorching hot water and then they were herded back into the cold until they froze to death.

Furthermore, when a healthy man was killed, Dr. Heidel, the camp's SS doctor, wrote *AKS-Allemeine Körperschwäche*, which was a general weakening of the body, known as *cachexia*, a disease from which the inmates often died. When the prisoners were hung, however, he attributed their demise to pneumonia and sometimes *Freitod*, suicide. Others were listed as an *Ex-Exekution*, performed, of course, in accordance with some *Gestapo* court decision. Lastly, the insurmountable corpses that had been rushed off to death in special trucks, trains, and chambers were denoted in the records by the initials S.B, *Sonder Behandlung*, special treatment. Despite the numerous categories, all the deceased were systematically marked with the letter T in the record books. T for *Tot*—dead, and were permanently crossed off. In all the camps, a modest six million were casually and indifferently marked *Tot* (dead) and with equal nonchalance erased. In any case, as time went on, the Nazis were especially careful to cover their tracks for fear that they were losing the war; an eventuality which became more and more evident.

By the beginning of the New Year, my job was simply now to take care of the dead. Many had been added to these work details, given that the typhus epidemic had taken on unforeseen proportions. The minute one of the inmates died, we disrobed him and wrote a number on his chest. Before we could turn around, his personal belongings were also immediately stolen. We stacked the corpses one on top of the other in a shed near the hospital, but since the shed was minuscule, the cadavers could never all fit. The bodies, themselves, were never considered of much interest, except, of course, for the SS, who were motivated by the eternal gold which was often to be found in the prisoner's teeth; the SS were reputed for inspecting the mouths of the dead inmates as they avariciously held their rusty pliers. Not surprisingly, only a fraction of the gold was turned into treasury.

Karren, sometimes drawn by the Russian prisoners of war, but more often by the most delinquent and brutal of the Polish political prisoners, were visible throughout the camp en route with the dead or near dead to the crematorium. On one of the larger *Karren*, we stuffed the corpses into a large black coffin, which had been made for three of them, but instead we often doubled the amount of cadavers. The remnants of their emaciated black and blue bodies stuck out of the coffins as a testimonial of the Nazis' total lack of humanity.

I soon believed I was living in some sort of twilight zone between the living and the dead. In this never-never land, block thirty, I soon realized, was the worst statement of Nazi victimization. This was the barrack where the most ill Jewish women were sent. By the middle of winter, when we were in the throes of the worst of the typhoid epidemic, the straw floor was now soaked with pus and excreta, the stench was so horrible that it was beyond description. Here, the women were no longer given food, but were left to die, completely unattended. Around eleven each morning even some of these *Muselmänner*, half alive, barely able to crawl, their glassy eyes sunken deep into their sockets and their bones protruding, were carted to the crematorium in one of the *Karren*. Others who were unquestionably dead were placed in piles outside the block.

Similarly, once a week, some other prisoners who were straddling a thin line between life and death, others who were in the infirmary and still in need of medical care, some who had been injured at work, and sometimes even some who were relatively healthy, were taken to Camp Four. Here, as in the hospital itself, or certainly hut thirty, no prisoners were brought back to health and were starved to death, not being given even a portion of bread. After having died of starvation and disease, they were taken in trucks and buried, in specially dug mass pits in the forest, where, reminiscent of *Kommando Stützpunkt*, a group of inmates doused the corpses with tar and burned them, flipping them once again with pitchforks, like devils contending with the witches on Walpurgis Night!

I was soon promoted, or demoted, whatever the case may be, to the crematory where I worked mainly with the Polish inmates like those who had been chosen for the driving of the *Karre*. These were among the most vicious Poles in camp. But by now, I felt completely comatose to both the living and the dead, so fortunately not much now affected me. In any case, like *Kommando Stützpunkt*, we were all slated to die. The crematory even for us was normally the last stop. However, with the progression of the war, the epidemic and the upcoming evacuation, the camp was in a state of upheaval, so the usual practices, fortunately for us, had not been maintained.

The only advantage about working in the crematory was that we were exempted from roll call, probably because our services were more indispensable than those of many of the other inmates. This notwithstanding, the roll call officers had not completely forgotten us and would shout over the public address to the convicts who worked in the crematory, "You birds in the crematory, get on with it and stick your heads out the windows!" Whereupon myself and the others understood that we should pick up a group of bodies and hold them out of the windows for the SS to inspect from afar. Within the crematory itself, the Poles were throwing many live bodies into the oven without giving it a second thought. They grabbed the cadavers any old way and shoved them in headfirst. If a corpse was too tall to fit in the oven, only the top part of the body was burned, the rest of the corpse being incinerated later. Additionally, the crematory released rosy and pale yellow smoke and all of the camp stunk like fried rubber.

I felt particularly disheartened when sometimes women arrived at the gate devastated by the death of some relative and wishing to possess their ashes. Whenever this occurred, I could always imagine that one of the women might have been my mother asking for my brother's remains and maybe soon mine or Svetlana's. They were obliged to pay about two hundred and thirty marks to cover the expenses of the ashes, for the urn, for packing and for postage. We were ordered to scoop up a few kilograms of ash from the common pile of ashes, which were later sent to the duped women in question. The Nazis managed to make money even on the deaths of the poor Jews! With them, there were certainly never any free lunches!

By now, for months Allied planes had flown over the camps without bombing either them or the tracks leading to them. It made me later wonder to what extent Roosevelt, as he proclaimed, was really our supporter. In any case, we could hear the motors of the American planes buzzing relentlessly like a hive of angry bees as they perched over the camp in three-tiered formation. Concurrently, the German planes flapped like owls, sometimes as low as the tops of the lofty snow-covered pines in order to avoid recognition by the others above them. American and Russian planes had already bombed Gdynia, Gdansk, Elblag and Bydgoszcz in nighttime attacks. Would we and the other camps, now, be next? We could only wonder. Meanwhile, at Stutthof, the Nazis were burning unyieldingly camp and hospital files in order to avoid all traces of their atrocities.

On January twenty-fourth, an announcement was made over the loudspeaker to the prisoners: "Be prepared to travel. Tomorrow at four o'clock in the morning, we're leaving". Within less than twenty-four hours, eleven thousand five hundred of the remaining close to twenty-four thousand prisoners formed columns, many accompanied by a sled. Each of the groups was assigned its escorts, consisting of a *Kommandant*, an SS NCO as well as forty guards, most of whom had been brought especially from Gdansk. Each of the columns was overseen by troops of SS, always with dogs as well as two machine guns and two special reserves. On the first day of the first evacuation, seven male and one female column departed on foot west for Gdansk where the prisoners were to be lodged. However, between the poor weather conditions and the masses of German civilians and retreating *Wehrmacht* units blocking the roads, the routing was changed and the seven day march became twelve. Just preceding their departure, each of the evacuated was given five hundred grams of bread and one hundred and twenty grams of margarine or cheese to last them for the first few days of their trip. During the twelve- day-march, they only received additional rations three times. Although a few of my women friends from Riga were among the women evacuated, most of the Jews, including myself, and those too ill to travel, were to leave later in the spring on the evacuation by sea—providing, of course, we survived through the arduous winter. Simultaneously, rumor also had it that the camp would be burned and those who remained murdered before the arrival of the Russians. Mother and Svetlana, who left from Sophienwalde later, recounted that, while sometimes they slept in barns and stables, at other times, very occasionally they marched even into the night. When the SS became impatient with the heavy snow and the twenty degree below weather and an inmate walked more slowly than the others, he was immediately shot, usually in the back of the head or the neck and left behind like an abandoned animal. Other than the systematic shots of the Germans, the only noise that could be heard in the still of the moonlit night was the consistent baying and whining of their bloodhounds as they tugged hysterically on their leashes. They later told me, too, how they waded knee deep in the snow, their rest stops lasting only fifteen minutes, they and the others having almost died of exhaustion. Otherwise, other Jewish friends later also told us that as they passed one German border town after another, they were extremely angered in fact by the predictable attitude of the Germans who stared at them with hostility as they marched by. In the towns, there were huge swastikas and portraits of Hitler interspersed throughout the walls. Afterwards, when they first arrived in Pomerania, despite the signs warning the people that, should they help the prisoners, they risked death, the Kashubians greeted them with warmth and generosity. As soon as the mayor of many of the towns received word of their approach, several kettles of potato and cabbage soup were prepared for their arrival. In the streets and along the road, they were greeted kindly by groups of bleak, awed eyed Polish women and children carrying the soup, while others stood empathetically with sandwiches, bread and even cake. It seemed that most of the men had been either mobilized or arrested. Many of the Poles were furthermore calling out the names of a family member, searching desperately for a missing wife or husband, brother or sister. They also despairingly threw bundles of blankets and warm clothing to the indigents as the SS cursed and cudgeled them aside. Both my mother and sister as well as many others believed that they survived this death march in great part due to the aid of the Kashubians. In any case, they and many of the other Jewish women found themselves after close to two weeks at Burgdorf, an already existing camp with the habitual minimal living conditions. Others were taken to former labour camps which were often even worse, many of which were comprised of farm buildings and barns without plumbing and not even the most rudimentary sanitation. Within the first month in these former labor camps equipped for only one hundred to two hundred, half of the five hundred to two thousand prisoners had died.

Meanwhile, Mother and Svetlana were liberated on May eighth while some of the neighboring towns were being bombed. They still speak about their amazement as they saw the sky illuminated with scattered dots while the smoke crept up to the heavens. Meanwhile, apart from the prisoners, they still remember even the flocks of sheep from a neighboring farm who crept aimlessly near them with a lost and melancholy look in their eyes as the animals bleated forlornly, equally uncertain of their fate.

By March, as there were large numbers of German troops surrounding Stutthof, heavily equipped with weapons and other forms of arms, the Russians thus began bombing the camp, which was admittedly extremely frightening. Furthermore, by the middle of April, Himmler's ultimatum was broadcast over the radio in Germany and German occupied countries: "Surrender is out of the question. No inmate can be captured alive by the enemy." This news was equally alarming.

Therefore, less than two weeks later, we were assembled for the second evacuation. By then, we were only three thousand three hundred remaining prisoners, almost half of us being Jews. Some of us were loaded like cattle into a narrow gauge train, while others were forced to walk and trudged wearily on a six-hour march along the Baltic seacoast, frozen to the bone by the biting sea wind. In the meantime, the SS cracked their whips and screamed pitilessly, *Schnell, schnell*! After a two-day wait on the Vistula shore at Nickelswalde, we were loaded on three river barges towed by tugboats which were to sail west. We were forced to board them through gangways, which were so narrow that many fell into the water and drowned. Another barge was also designated for the approximately five hundred women deadly ill with typhus. This "quarantine" motor barge carried a yellow flag in order to show it was transporting diseased people. This boat also sailed west, but not surprisingly, was never heard of or seen again.

The barges were actually too decrepit for use and were overloaded to the point that it seemed that at any moment they might sink. Reminiscent of our trip to Stutthof, we were immediately rushed down a metal ladder leading down to the hold, covered by damp, filthy and smelling straw. We were given no food, not even drinking water. In fact, all we had to drink was some disgusting liquid, a strange mixture of rain and seawater that lay on the bottom of the hold beneath the straw. Meanwhile, we also chewed on the straw like famished horses as we listened to the German crew above, screaming down at us with degradation: "You cows! You pigs! Lets see you die like filthy swine". In the hold, we were also accompanied by the Polish and Ukrainian inmates who had previously attended to the manual labor at the camp. Now, their main role was to throw us Jews overboard when we were dead and often when we were still alive. To them, it was of little importance. Actually, I kept asking myself why the Germans had not just killed all of us a long time ago, instead of endlessly drawing out all this torture. Finally, I realized they must have relished in our endless suffering.

Anyhow, by early May, most of the coast had been overtaken by the British, whose planes roared like hungry lions in the sky. Then, if you can imagine, on the last day of the war a British bomb exploded near us, damaging and setting fire to our barge. With alacrity, the German took charge, screaming out emphatically: "*Die Juden ins Wasser* !" (Jews into the water!), continuing: "*Das Schiff ist zu schwer* !" (The ship is too heavy!), the

Germans, aided by the Polish and Ukrainian inmates, joyfully pushing as many Jews as possible overboard. Those happy few who were spared, myself among them, were saved by a nearby British ship and taken to Stettin.

Several weeks following liberation, some of the Jewish relief agencies gathered the survivors' names and published them. Every time a list was released, I checked for Mother's or Svetlana's name, but to no avail. I was heartbroken. During this period, after having hitchhiked to Magdeburg, I broke into an apartment there that had belonged to a German who was either missing in action or somewhere in hiding. My motivation, like many of the other refugees was twofold. On the one hand, I needed to find a place to live, on the other, I was seeking revenge.

Meanwhile, the order came from Moscow that all Soviet citizens, such as myself, were to return to their hometowns. Haunted by nightmarish memories, there was no way I was willing to return to Riga and to Russian rule. I sought the aid of the Jewish *Gemeinde* in Magdeburg which helped me get to Berlin, now occupied by the Russians, the British, the Americans and even the French. The *Gemeinde* agency gave me one of their travel passes to Berlin which they signed and stamped with their official seal. While I took the train there and was engrossed in one of the local newspapers, suddenly we made an unexpected stop and half a dozen Russian soldiers mounted the car in order to examine our travel documents. I went through a moment of sheer panic, terrified that although my papers were apparently in order, I might still be arrested because one of the soldiers would realize that I was a Latvian Jew and not a Viennese Jew as the agency had falsified.

When I finally arrived in the capital, I went to the Berlin refugee shelter in Schlachtensee in order to seek asylum from the communists. There, most of the people were also Jews, mainly on their way to the United States or Palestine. In this UNRRA camp, I miraculously found some of my school comrades from Riga, but unfortunately none had any news of my family members. As was almost inevitably the case, they themselves had no remaining relatives, all of them having been killed in the war. In any case, the camp's priority was to assist all of us in being transported to one of the Allied occupied sections of Germany. It was also through this organization, combined with the Red Cross, that I was enabled to find my Mother as well as relatives living in America. They later sent the necessary affidavit in which they assured all financial support which would allow our entry into the United States.

I once learned in America that Svetlana had been hospitalized soon after the war for *cachexia*, at which time she was separated from Mother. Afterwards, she told us that she had been picked up by the police in Hamburg as a youngster in distress and brought to the Warburg Estate which was located in the exclusive Hamburg suburb of Blankenese. The Warburg banking family had donated their palatial mansion to aid some fifty Jewish youths to rehabilitate themselves after the war. The estate, itself, occupied somewhere between fifteen to twenty acres on the Elbe and was comprised of roughly twenty-five rooms and even an elevator. Anyway, the children there ranged from twelve to sixteen and besides their normal schooling, their studies were mainly focused on teaching them the necessary strategy for entering Palestine illegally by evading the British controls. In the meantime, our relatives from the United States were constantly indulging Svetlana not only by sending her money, but also cigarettes which were invaluable for any form of "exchange". Ironically, she was thus soon living in the lap of luxury with even her own chauffeur for herself and her new friends. Although she missed us, she later admitted that she had very mixed feelings about her ultimate departure over a year later from the Warburg Estate, and even Germany itself. It was, not surprisingly, difficult for her to leave her fairy tale existence where she had gone from rags to riches. I must admit to you that I could not help feeling a bit envious, if not jealous.

Over a year and a half after liberation, the liberty-class boats, which used to carry the troops during the war, now entered the port at Bremer Hafen to take us to the United States. By now we had received documents and were no longer regarded as refugees but had acquired the status of full-fledged members of the community.

I remember so well arriving on the dock with Mother in order to board the ship leaving for America. After an agent inspected all our documents and verified that our names were on the departure list, a blue badge was pinned on our jackets on which were written the letters "HIAS" (Hebrew Immigrant Aid Society in English and in Yiddish as well as an inscription, "Bremen 1947"). Another agent gave us each a ten-dollar bill for spending money during our passage. After leaving a sack containing a few of my personal items on my bunk bed, I joined Mother and the others in the recreation room and actively participated in the games and danced the jitterbug with them, while the ship hooted its final adieu. However, even though I seemed to share the others joy and optimism in my life-long journey to the "Golden Land", I was in reality deeply reticent, filled with anxiety, not knowing on any level what to expect. I was further overwhelmed with nostalgia for a past, for a people and for a family I could never forget.

DÜSSELDORF

More than thirty years after the end of the war, I flew to Düsseldorf, accompanied by my old friend Dr Gertrude Schneider, who had since written about the life in the Riga ghetto, Kaiserwald and Stutthof as well as about the fate of her fellow Austrian Jews. She too had been asked to testify regarding the various murders at Kaiserwald. We both felt the utter obligation to participate in the trial, yet we admitted to re-opening unbelievably bitter wounds. As many others of the survivors, we also never really quite understood how we had remained alive and most of our family members had not. At times, we, along with so many others, found ourselves overwhelmed by guilt, which we could only attempt to understand or to rationalize.

Although Düsseldorf, itself, had been coined by Napoleon as the "little Paris", I remember Fräulein telling me that it had never been endowed with the gentle grace of Munich nor the importance as an artistic center of Cologne. Yet, due to the artistic patronage of Jan Wellen, as of the eighteenth century it still became well known for its artists, writers, and musicians. Heinrich Heine was born and spent his youth there, while Brahms, Mendelssohn, Schumann, Goethe, and even the painter Peter Cornelius, had lived and worked there. Of these talents, Germany could at least be proud!

Preparing myself for the opening of the trial, I walked up and down the Kö for the first time in almost fifty years. The little I had learned from Fräulein about Düsseldorf's personalities was all I had left to console me. Time seemed to have passed so quickly and with it so much unexpected tragedy. Suddenly, I missed Abrasha terribly, even Fräulein, all of them, Mother, Father. As one hour followed another, I re-lived some of my first anti-Semitic experiences as a young boy. Consequently, I decided to never contact any of the German branch of my family. I was convinced that my cousins were still staunch Nazis. Maybe they would not have even remembered me and Abrasha? And if they had not forgotten us, maybe they would have been pleased to learn that one more Jew had been killed by the Nazis, even if he was a member of their own family? Anything was possible.

The next morning, Gertrude and I left our hotel and walked down to the port in order to get our bearings, before the trial. As we walked past Hundertwasser's overpowering, futuristic metalized towers standing up arrogantly near the Rhine, we realized that the Germany we had so come to hate was now turning away from its remorse-ridden past and looking instead toward a mechanized future devoid of all souvenirs.

Not long, after, we walked into the courthouse where I saw Wisner for the first time since that rainy evening of my brother's selection. I tried to control myself, but to no avail. I began shaking and in an ungovernable rage screamed out "You fucking murderer". I walked toward him and was held back by two guards, otherwise I might have killed him. All my anger which had been pent up for close to a lifetime was projected onto him. He hid his face in fear and shame in his hands and awaited the inevitable verdict a few weeks later.[32]

> *Help me, Doctor. As you know, I have tried to remain as optimistic as possible despite the fact that the camps still haunt me day and night, night and day. As a proud family man with a loving wife and three sons and as an esteemed career diplomat, I have attempted to re-integrate myself into society. Apparently—but only apparently—I have succeeded in transcending and enduring all my past adversity. I still need your help to reconcile myself to the hellish and demonic potential of mankind which I witnessed as an adolescent and which revisited me upon again confronting Heinz Wisner.*

---

32 See American Jewish Committee, 1987, p. 247

BIBLIOGRAPHY

Addison, Lucy. *Letters from Latvia*. London: Macdonald, 1986.

American Jewish Committee. *American Jewish Yearbook, 1987*. New York: The Jewish Publication Society of America, 1987.

Benton, Peggy. *Baltic Countdown*. London: Centaur, 1984.

Bettelheim, Bruno. *The Informed Heart; autonomy in a mass age*. Glencoe, Ill: Free Press, 1960

Bobe, Mendel. The *Jews in Latvia*. Tel Aviv: Ben Nun Press, 1973.

Bousfield, Jonathan. *The Baltic States: Estonia, Latvia and Lithuania*. New York: Rough Guides, 2004.

Breitman, Richard. *The Architect of Genocide: Himmler and the Final Solution*. London: Bodley Head, 1991.

Burleigh, Michael and Wolfgang Wippermann. *The Racial State: Germany, 1933-1945*. Cambridge: Cambridge University Press, 1991.

Cohen, Elie. *Human Behavior in the Concentration Camp*. London: Free Association Books, 1988.

Conan, Eric. *Sans oublier les enfants*. Paris : Bernard Grasset, 1991.

Dawidowicz, Lucy S. *The War against the Jews*. New York: Rinehart and Winston, 1975.

des Pres, Terrence. *The Survivor: An Anatomy of Life in the Death Camps*. New York: Oxford University Press, 1976.

Dobroszycki, Lucjan and Jeffrey S. Gurock. *The Holocaust in the Soviet Union*. London: M.E. Sharpe, 1993.

Drywa, Danuta. *The Extermination of Jews in Stutthof Concentration Camp. 1939-1945*. Gdansk: Panstwowe Museum Stutthof, 2001.

Dwork, Deborah. *Children with a Star: Jewish Youth in Nazi Europe*. New Heaven and London: Yale University Press, 1991.

Eder, Cyril. *Les Comtesses de la Gestapo*. Paris: Bernard Grasset, 2006.

Eisenberg, Azriel. *The Lost Generation: Children in the Holocaust*. New York: Pilgrim Press, 1982.

Eksteins, Modris. *Walking Since Daybreak: a story of Eastern Europe, World War II and the Heart of Our Century*. Boston: Houghton Mifflin Co., 1999.

Englelmann, Bernt. *In Hitler's Germany: daily life in the Third Reich*. New York: Pantheon Books, 1986.

Ezergailis, Andrew. *Nazi/ Soviet Disinformation about the Holocaust in Nazi-Occupied Latvia: Daugavas Vanagi: who are they ? –Revisited*. Riga: 2005.

——*The German Occupation of Latvia 1941-1945: What did America know?* Riga: Historical Institute of Latvia, 2002.

——*The Holocaust in Latvia, 1941-1944: the missing Center*. Riga: Historical Institute of Latvia, 1996.

Forsyth, Frederick. *The Odessa File*. London: Arrow Books, Ltd., 1972.

Friedrich, Otto. *Before the Deluge: A Portrait of Berlin in the 1920's*. New York: Harper and Row, 1972.

Fromm, Bella. *Blood & Banquets: A Berlin Social Diary*. New York: Carol Publishing Group, 1990.

Gawsewitch, Jean-Claude. *Le Grand Livre Des Témoins*. Paris : Ramsay, 1995.

Gerson, Werner. *Le nazisme, société secrète*. Paris : Pierre Belfond, 1976.

Gill, Anton. *A Dance Between Flames : Berlin Between the Wars*. London: Abacus, 1995.

Gimutas, Marijas. *The Balts*. London: Thames and Hudson, 1963.

Gordon, Frank. *Latvians and Jews: Between Germany and Russia*. Stockholm: Memento, 1990.

Grabowska-Chalka, Janina. *Stutthof Guide*. Gdansk: MW, 2004.

Grunberger, Richard. *A Social History of the Third Reich*. London: Weidenfeld and Nicolson, 1971.

Grunfeld, Frede. V. *The Hitler File: A Social History of Germany and the Nazis*. New York: Random House, 1974.

Hamann, Brigitte. *Hitler's Vienna: A Dictator's Apprenticeship*. New York: Oxford University Press, 1999.

Haste, Cate. *Nazi Women: Hitler's seduction of a nation*. London: Channel 4, 2001.

Hilberg, Raul. *The Destruction of the European Jews*. New York: Harper and Row, 1961.

Hitler's Table-Talk. Oxford: Oxford University Press, 1953.

Hoffmann, Heinrich. *Hitler was My Friend*. London: Burke Publishing Co., Ltd., 1955.

Iwens, Sidney. *How Dark the Heavens: 1400 Days in the Grip of Nazi Terror*. New York: Shengold Publishers, Inc., 1990.

Kacel, Boris. *From Hell to Redemption: A Memoir of the Holocaust*. Niwot, Colorado: University Press of Colorado, 1998.

Kehr, Helen and Janet Langmaid, comps. *The Nazi Era 1919-1945: A Select Bibliography of Published Works from the Early Roots to 1980*. London: Mansell Publishing Limited, 1982.

Kennan, George F. *Memoirs 1925-1950*. New York: Pantheon, 1983.

Kershaw, Ian. *Hitler, 1889-1936: hubris*. New York: WW Norton, 1999.

——*"The Hitler myth": image and reality in the Third Reich*. Oxford: Clarendon Press, 1987.

Kersten, Felix. *The Memoirs of Doctor Felix Kersten*. New York: Doubleday and Co., 1947.

Kessel, Joseph. *The Man with the Miraculous Hands*. New York: Farrar, Straus and Cudahy, 1961.

Klee, Ernst et al, eds. *"The Good Old Days": The Holocaust as Seen by its Perpetrators and Bystanders*. New York: Konecky & Konecky, 1988.

Kogon, Eugen. *The Theory and Practice of Hell: The German Concentration Camps and the System Behind Them*. New York: Farrar, Straus and Giroux, 1950.

Knopp, Guido. *Hitler's Women*. New York: Routledge, 2003.

Kubizek, August. *The Young Hitler I knew*. London: Green Hill Books, 2006.

Kuodyte, Dalia and Rimantas Stankevicius, comps. *Whoever saves one life: the efforts to save Jews in Lithuania between 1941 and 1944*. Vilnius: Genocide and Resistance Center of Lithuania, 2006.

Levinson, Isaac. *The Untold Story*. Johannesburg: Kayor Publishing House, 1958.

Lewis, Wyndham. *The Hitler Cult*. London: Dent, 1939.

Lifton, Robert J. *The Nazi Doctors: Killing and the Psychology of Genocide*, 1986.

Ludecke, Kurt G.W. *I Knew Hitler*. New York: Scribner's, 1937.

Lukas, John. *June 1941: Hitler and Stalin*. New Haven, Connecticut: Yale University Press, 2006.

——*The Hitler of History*. New York: Knopf, 1997.

Michelson, Frida. *I Survived Rumbuli*. New York: Holocaust Library, 1979.

Michelson, Max. *City of Life City of Death: Memories of Riga*. Boulder, Colorado: University Press of Colorado, 2001.

Mitscherlich, Alexander and Fred Mielke. *Doctors of Infamy: The Story of the Nazi Medical Crimes*. New York: Schuman, 1949.

Mosse, George L. *Nazi Culture*. Madison, Wisconsin: University of Wisconsin Press, 1966.

Otten, Karl. *A Combine of Aggression: Masses, elite and dictatorship in Germany*. London: Allen and Unwin, 1942.

Plakans, Andrejs. *The Latvians: A Short History*. Stanford: Hoover Institute Press, 1995.

Reynolds, Quentin, et al. *Minister of Death*. New York: Viking, 1960.

Rolnikas, Macha. *Je devais le raconter*. Paris: Les Editeurs Français réunis, 1966.

Praise for the French edition of
BEHIND THE BARBED WIRE

In part an historical account, in part a psychological novel, the narrator of this subtle work relates to his psychiatrist his unique existence as a Lettonian Jew who initially visits pre-war Nazi Germany and who is later incarcerated in the ghetto and the camps. With this book, Gwendolyn Chabrier succeeds in winning a difficult bet.

Florence Noiville, *Le Monde*

Gwendolyn Chabrier has constructed a psychological novel which is tragically hypnotic.

Le Figaro Magazine

Author, doctor of literature, Faulkner specialist, Gwendolyn Chabrier succeeds in rendering this voyage into the Nazi atrocity, both historical and psychological. This work sheds new light on the Holocaust.

Valérie Trierweiler, *Paris Match*

Behind the Barbed Wire is inspired by the author's forty year friendship with George Schwab, a Lettonian Holocaust survivor. This work is a psychological novel, partially a testimonial, partially an account of an unknown facet of the Holocaust, the extermination of some 70,000 Lettonian Jews.

Marianne Payot, *L'Express*

After much research and travel to Lettonia, Gwendolyn Chabrier knew how to transcribe the unimaginable and Nazi cynicism without falling into the trap of the cliché or facile pity. Her latest book is strong and captivating.

Le Dauphiné Libéré

An historical novel, a psychological novel or pure history? Gwendolyn Chabrier has always had the gift of presenting the world and those who populate it in both a unique and original way.

Bernard Delattre, *Dernieres Nouvelles d'Alsace*

Schneider, Gertrude. *Exile and Destruction : the fate of the Austrian Jews, 1938-1945.* Westport, Connecticut: Praeger Publishers, 1995.

——*Journey into Terror: Story of the Riga Ghetto.* New York: Praeger Publishers, 2001.

——*Muted Voices: Jewish Survivors of Latvia Remember.* New York: Philosophical Library, Inc., 1987.

——Romance in the Ghetto. *Jewish Daily Forward.* Oct. 19, 1980, section B: 1-10.

——Salaspils: The Story of an Extermination Camp. *The Jewish Press* No.15 (1985) : 24.

——The Jews of Riga. *Jewish Frontier.* 42.3(1975) : 15-20.

Seligman, Ruth. *"Libau: The Town that Never Died."* Midstream 32.9 (1986) : 38-39.

Shalit, Dov. *They were Numbers. A true Story of a Holocaust survivor as seen by a child. 1939-1945.* Ramat Hasharon, Israel, 2002.

Shirer, William L. *The Rise and Fall of the Third Reich: A History of Nazi Germany.* New York: Simon and Schuster, 1959.

——*Berlin Diary: The Journal of a Foreign Correspondent, 1934-1941.* New York: Alfred A. Knopf, 1941.

Sruoga, Balys. *Forest of the Gods.* Vilnius: Versus Aureus Publishers, Ltd, 2005.

Swain, Geoff. *Between Stalin and Hitler.* New York: Routledge, 2001.

Taylor, Telford. *Sword and Swastika.* New York: Simon and Schuster, 1952.

The Goebbels Diary. New York: Doubleday and Co., 1948.

The Hidden and Forbidden History of Latvia Under Soviet and Nazi Occupations 1940-1991. Riga: Institute of the History of Latvia, 2005.

The Jews in Riga. Riga: The Museum and Documentation Center of the Latvian Society of Jewish Culture, 1991.

Todorov, Tzvetan. *Facing the Extreme: moral life in the Concentration Camps.* New York: Metropolitan Books, 1996.

Trevor-Roper, H.R. *The Last Days of Hitler*. New York: The Macmillan Co., 1947.

Valentin, Veit. *The German People: their history and civilization from the Holy Roman Empire to the Third Reich*. New York: A.A Knopf, 1951.

Waite, Robert G.L. *The Psychopathic God: Adolf Hitler*. New York: Basic Books, 1977.

About the Author

Dr. Gwendolyn Chabrier graduated *magna cum laude* from New York University with a BA and MA. She began her doctoral studies at Harvard, which were completed in France, where she was awarded the Doctorat d'Etat degree with highest honors from the Université de Paris IV-Sorbonne.

Dr. Chabrier has been a professor of literature at New York University, the University of Rouen, and the Sorbonne. She has also been a literary scout for Les Editions Lebaud in Paris. She is the author of three previous works published in both English and French:

Faulkner's Families: a Southern Saga

An Asian Destiny

Norman Mailer: The Self-Appointed Messiah

www.ingramcontent.com/pod-product-compliance
Lightning Source LLC
Chambersburg PA
CBHW032128160426
43197CB00008B/556